SCIENCE NOTEBOOK

CLASS -X (CGBSE)

TUSHAR RANJAN DEY

Made with ♥ on the Notion Press Platform

www.notionpress.com

To my family who supported me while writing this book.
To my mentors and students who motivated me.

CONTENT

ACKNOWLEDGEMENT

For Content Reference
Cgbse Text Book
Ncert
Internet/Google
Ai Tools
For Image -
Brgfx / Freepik, Image: Freepik.Com".,
Blastlabels.Jpg: J Navas,
Designed By Pikisuperstar / Freepik"

Preface

Welcome to the "Success Point Science Guide for Class 10th"! This book is crafted to simplify science and help you grasp key concepts effectively. Each chapter is designed to build on your knowledge, presenting clear explanations, diagrams, examples, and exerci ses to enhance learning.

Our guide includes practice problems, exam tips, and real-life applications, making science both engaging and practical. The insights and strategies f rom our experienced educators aim to help you excel academically.

We're excited to be part of your learning journey and hope this guide inspires curiosity and a deeper appreciation for science.

Happy Learning!

Chapter -1

1. Choose the correct answer-

(i) Name the process through which modern breed of pet dog was acquired- (a) Natural selection (c) Juvenile selection (b) Artificial selection (d) Work selection

(ii) (ii) Forelimbs of dog and sheep are for walking, whale for swimming and that of bat for flying. All these are examples of- (a) Analogous (c) Undeveloped organ (b) Homologous (d) all above Evolution 13

(iii) Which of the following are analogous structures- (a) Wings of bat and butterfly (b) Gills of prawn and fish (c) Thorns of bougainvillea and tendrils of bottle gourd (d) Wings of bat and legs of horse

(iv) While proposing his theory, Darwin was influenced by- (a) The observations of his voyage (b) Cell theory (c) Law of genetics of Mendel (d) None of the above

ANS:- (i) b (ii) b (iii) a (iv) a

2. Fill in the blanks

(i) A group of organisms which can interbreed sexually producing viable off-springs is known as ....

(ii) Difference among beaks of finches show the .... among them.

(iii) Some bacteria can grow in the medium containing streptomycin (antibiotic). The reason behind this is ....

ANS:- (i) biological species (ii) homologous (iii) diversity (iv)variation

4. Write two difference between natural and artificial selection.

Ans:-

Natural selection	Artificial selection
Nature chooses which traits are best for survival. The environment plays a big role.	Humans choose which traits they want in plants or animals, like breeding dogs for specific looks.
Helps organisms adapt to their environment over a long time, increasing diversity in nature	Changes traits quickly, but can sometimes cause health problems or reduce variety among species.

5. What do we come to know from the theory of evolution as proposed by Darwin and Wallace?

Ans:- The theory of evolution as proposed by Darwin and Wallace . It emphasizes that all organisms share a common ancestry and have evolved through processes like natural selection and adaptation. This understanding provides a framework for studying the complexities of life, illustrating how species respond to environmental challenges and how new species arise. Ultimately, the theory of evolution offers a cohesive explanation for the diversity of life and our place within the natural world.

6. What are the main points of the theory of evolution of organisms?
Ans:- The main points of the theory of evolution of organisms

- Common Ancestry: All living organisms are descended from a common ancestor, indicating a shared lineage
- Natural Selection: Traits that enhance survival and reproduction become more common in a population over generations. This process is often referred to as "survival of the fittest."
- Variation: Individuals within a species show variations in traits, and these variations can be inherited. Genetic differences arise through mutations and recombination.
- Adaptation: Over time, populations adapt to their environments, leading to changes in traits that help them thrive in specific conditions.
- Speciation: New species can arise when populations become isolated and evolve independently, often due to changes in their environment or behaviour.
- Gradual Change: Evolution typically occurs gradually over long periods, although it can also happen more rapidly under certain conditions.

7. What is the role of selection and adaptation in the process of evolution?
Ans:- Role of Selection and Adaptation in Evolution
1. Selection:
Natural Selection: Favours individuals with traits that enhance survival and reproduction, leading to those traits becoming more common in the population.
Survival of the Fittest: Refers to how well an organism can adapt and reproduce in its environment.
Sexual Selection: Involves traits that increase mating success, influencing the prevalence of certain characteristics.
2. Adaptation
Environmental Fit: Adaptation involves changes in traits that help organisms survive in specific environments, like thicker fur in cold climates.
Long-Term Changes: Over generations, adaptations can lead to significant changes and even the development of new species.
Dynamic Process: Adaptation is ongoing, as organisms must continually adjust to changing environments to survive.

Extra question

1) explain analogous and homologous characteristics?

Ans:- 1. Analogous Characteristics Traits that have similar functions but arise from different evolutionary backgrounds and do not share a common ancestor (e.g., wings of birds and insects).
2. Homologous Characteristics: Traits that share a common ancestry and have similar structures but may serve different functions in different species (e.g., forelimbs of humans, whales, and bats).

Chapter -2

Text book question: -

1)Why is pickle not stored in copper, aluminium container?

Ans. Pickle is not stored in copper and aluminium containers to prevent it from acidity and basicity because its pH value gets changed.

Q. 2. A small amount of vegetable fell in Kusum's clothes during lunch. After going home, she applied soap on that area, then the cloth became red. Explain its cause.

Ans. Soaps are fatty salts, that react with vegetable juice and act as acid-base indicator, which changes colour.

Q. 3. Suresh is a blind student. Which indicators can he used to identify acid and base?

Ans.- By using olfactory indicators.

Q. 4. Explain the reaction of metals with dilute hydrochloric acid by an example.

Ans. Reaction of metals with dilute hydrochloric acid is known as displacement reaction. For example: Reaction of hydrochloric acid with zinc metal.

$$2HCl\ (aq) + zn(s) \rightarrow ZnCl_2(aq) + H_2$$

Q. 5. Write balanced chemical equation for the reaction of Calcium hydrogen carbonate with hydrochloric acid.

Ans. $Ca(HCO_3)_2 + 2HCl \rightarrow CaCl_2 + 2H_2O + 2CO_2$

Q. 6. Non-metallic oxides are acidic in nature. Give example.

Ans. Non-metallic oxide reacts with base and form salt and water, therefore they are acidic in nature. Example:

$SO_2 + 2NaOH\ (aq) \longrightarrow Na_2SO_3 + H_2O$

Q. 7. Identify the acid in the following: HNO_3, Na_2CO_3, HCl

Ans. Acid: HNO_3 and HCl.

Q. 8. Sulphuric acid is a strong acid and ammonium hydroxide is a weak base. Explain.

Ans. The strength of an acid or a base depends on the extent of its ionisation. H_2SO_4 (Sulphuric acid) separates H^+ ion completely in water, therefore, it is a strong acid, whereas NH_4OH (Ammonium hydroxide) gives OH^- ion which ionise partially, thus it behaves like a weak base.

Q. 9. When a few pieces of sodium hydroxide (NaOH) are placed on dry red litmus paper, then initially there is no change in colour, but after some time its colour starts becoming blue. Explain the cause.

Ans.- Sodium hydroxide. (NaOH) is dry initially therefore it does not change the colour Later it absorbs moisture and becomes wet Therefore, it changes red litmus blue.

Q. 10. Glucose and starch do not show acidic property in aqueous solution, whereas sulphuric and acetic acid do, Explain the reason.

Ans. Sulphuric acid and acetic acid dissolve in water and release hydrogen (H+) ion, which is acidic. But glucose and starch do not release H+ ion. Therefore, both of these are not acidic.

Q. 11. Are H (aq) ions present in basic solution, if yes, then why is the solution basic?
Ans. Due to more number of OH- ion in the solution than H+ ion, the solution is basic.
Q. 12. You have two aqueous solution 'A' and 'B'. pH value of solution 'A' is 6 and pH value of solution 'B' is 8. In which of the solution H+ ion concentration is more? Among them which of the solution is acidic and which is basic?
Ans. H+ ion concentration will be more in solution 'A' therefore it will be acidic, where as in solution 'B' H+ ion concentration will be less• Thus, it will be basic.
Q. 13. Julie identified five solutions A, C, D and E by universal indicator, when pH value obtained were 9, 7, 1, 13 and 6. On this basis, state which solution is:
(a) Weakly acidic, (b) Weakly basic, (c) Strongly acidic, (d) Strong basic, (e) Neutral.

Ans. Properties of solution:	Weak acid	E solution
	Weak base	A solution
	Strong acid	C solution
	Strong base	D solution
	Neutral	B solution.

Q. 15. Identify the acidic and basic radicals in the following salts :
NH_4Cl, KNO_3, $(NH_4)_2CO_3$, $CuSO_4$.
Ans. Acidic Radicals :
Basic Radicals : NH4+ , K+ and Cu2+
Q. 16. What will be the nature of aqueous Potassium chloride solution ? Explain.
Ans. Aqueous solution of Potassium chloride is of neutral nature, because it is a salt of a strong acid (HCI) and strong base (KOH) which ionize completely. Due to same amount of H+ and OH-, aqueous KCI solution is neutral.
Exercise
1) Choose the correct option ··· ···
(i) In lemon juice: –
(a) H+ ions are more, OH– ions are less (b) H+ ions are less, OH– ions are more
(c) H+ ions and OH– ions are equal (d) Only H+ ions are present.
Ans: – Option (a).
(ii) When an acid reacts with a metal carbonate then we get
(a) Salt and water (b) Salt and water and carbon dioxide
(c) Salt and sulphur dioxide (d) Salt and hydrochloric acid are.
Ans: – Option (b).

(iii) Which among the following is not a strong acid
(a)HCl (b) HNO3
(c) CH_3COOH (d) H_2SO_4.

Ans: – Option (c).

(iv) The pH of a neutral solution is

(a) 1 (b) 0

(c) 14 (d) 7.

Ans: – option (d) 7.

(v) Sakina has a burning sensation in her stomach due to acidity; she needs. : ··· ···

(a) A strong acid (b) A strong base

(c) A weak base (d) A weak acid.

Ans: – option (b) A strong base.

(vi) The cause of tooth decay is pH of saliva

(a) Being less than 6.5 (b) Becoming 7

(c) Being less than 5.5 (d) Being more than 6.5.

Ans: – option (c).

(vii) Which of the following salts is acidic in nature

NaCl (b) Na_2SO_4 (c) NH_4Cl (d) KNO_3. ··· ···

Ans: – Option (c).

2) Write the names of any two acids found in the food that we eat.

Ans: – The acid which present in the food that we eat is citric acid of lemon and lactic acid in milky product.

3) How do we distinguish between acids and bases using an olfactory indicator? Ans: – In an olfactory indicator there used vanilla or onion extract which after the reaction with acid the sound is vanished but with the reaction with bases there are no changes in the smell which clearly distinguished between the acid and base.

4) The pH of fresh milk is 6. What will be the pH when it sets into curd/yogurt? Ans: – The PH of the milk decreases while it sets into curd. The PH is decrease as lactic acid is formed from milk. And the PH range of this lactic acid or yogurt is 7 4.5 to 5.5.

5) You have been given three test tubes. One of them has distilled water and of the remaining two, one has an acid and the second has a basic solution. If you only have red litmus paper then how will how identify the nature of solutions in each of the test tubes?

Ans: –. In the presence of base red litmus will change to blue and then putting it in acid it will change to red then putting it to distilled water no changes happen in its colour.

6) During an experiment, Neelam and Manish added concentrated sulphuric acid to dry (anhy-drous) sodium chloride. A gas evolved during the reaction. When Manish placed a dry bluelitmus paper near the mouth of the test tube nothing happened but when he placed a moistblue litmus paper, it became red. Explain why. ··· ···

Ans: – When Neelam and Manish added concentrated H_2SO_4 to dry NaCl then hydrogen chloride gas is produces.

$H_2SO_4 + NaCl \rightarrow HCl + Na_2SO_4$;

This hydrogen chloride gas when came in contact to wet litmus it becomes red but when it came in contact with dry litmus it doesn't show any changes.

7) Some substances and their pH values are given in the table. Analyse the data in the table and answer the following questions: Substance PH value Solution of baking soda Lemon juice 8.2 2.2 vinegar Sodium hydroxide 5.5 13 water

(a) Which of the substances are basic in nature?

(b) Which of the substances are acidic in nature?

(c) Which of the substances are neutral?

Ans: – (a) From the upper table we can say baking soda and sodium hydroxide has the PH value above 7 so these are basic in nature.

(b) In the table lemon juice and vinegar are acidic in nature as their PH value is under 7

(c) As water has PH value of 7 it is neutral in nature.

8)Acid's "A" and "B" were taken in two beakers. Acid "A" ionizes partially in water while acid "B" ionizes completely. On this basis, tell:

(a) Which among "A" and "B" is strong acid and which is weak?

(b) What is a weak acid?

(c) What is a strong acid?

(d) Give examples of both strong and weak acids.

Ans: – (a) As the acid a is ionized partially in water it is weak acid. And the acid B is ionized completely it is strong acid.

(b) A weak acid doesn't dissolve or ionized property in water. In the upper experiment the A is weak acid as it doesn't ionize completely. Example: – Acetic acid.

(c) If any acid completely ionized in a water solution, then that acid will be called a strong acid. Example: – Nitric acid.

(d) A strong acid is HCl or hydrochloric acid, nitric acid (HNO_3) and a weak acid is CH_3COOH or acetic acid.

9) Which gas is usually displaced during reaction between acids and a metal? How will you test this gas? Take the example of magnesium metal to explain.

Ans: – In a reaction between metal and acids salt and hydrogen gas is produced.

Metal + acid → salts + hydrogen;

By splint test we can assure that it is a hydrogen gas.

Example: – $Mg + 2HCl \rightarrow MgCl_2 + H_2$;

10) When an egg shell is reacted with dilute hydrochloric acid, foaming is observed and an effervescent gas is produced. Once foaming subsides, a lighted agarbatti is extinguished on placing it inside test tube. Explain the following in the given activity:

(a) Procedure or steps followed in the activity

(b) Draw the picture of the experimental set-up

(c) Write the balanced chemical equation of the reaction taking place.

Ans: – The steps which are take while doing this experiment are

(a) 5ml of 20% HCl solution are taken in a test tube. Egg shell of some amount are poured in the test tube. Now when we place any agarbatti in mouth of the test tube we seen that agarbatti ame is extinguished.

(b)

(c) The balanced chemical reaction is: $CaCO_3 + 2HCl \rightarrow CaCl_2 + CO_2 + H_2O$;

11) The pH of soil in Tikeshweri's eld is 4.2. How can she control the pH of her soil so that shegets a good paddy crop?

Ans: – The soil is seen clearly acidic in nature so for the control of the PH of the soil she must add some basic substance. So basic substance like calcium hydroxide ($Ca(OH)_2$) can be added.

12) What is neutralization reaction? Explain and give two examples.

Ans: – When after reaction between acid and base makes the product water and salt then this reaction can call neutralization reaction.

Example: – HCl (acid) + NaOH (base) → NaCl (salt) + H_2O;

13) Samaru added baking soda to raw milk so that its pH changed from 6 to 8. This milk will takelonger to change into curd; why?

Ans: – After adding the baking soda to the milk the solution become basic. As the baking soda made the solution to the PH of 8 which is basic in nature this milk takes some times to form curd. For this phenomenon to forming curd time is needed.

14) What is a salt? How is the nature of a salt determined? Take NH_4NO_3 and Na_2CO_3 asexamples and explain.

Ans: – The reaction between the acid and base produce salts and water. If any reaction acid is strong then the salt is acidic in nature and if the base is strong then the salt is basic in nature. The NH_4NO_3 is salt which is acidic in nature as at the time of producing this salt acid solution was more powerful whereas for producing the basic salts like Na_2CO_3 the solution was more basic in nature.

Chapter -3

TEXT-BOOK QUESTIONS

Q. 1. Water is sprinkled to extinguish spark of fire, why?

Ans. Heat capacity of water is high, when water is sprinkled, heat comes out due to which fire can easily be controlled. That is why water is sprinkled to extinguish spark of fire.

Q. 2. If 487•5 J of heat is required to the temperature of 25-gram copper from 25^0C to 75^0C, then what will be the specific heat of copper in J/g^0C?

sol.: -

Given, m = 25 gm, ΔT = 75-25 = 500C,

Q = 487.5 J Using Q = m SΔT

$$S = \frac{Q}{m\,\Delta T}$$

$$= \frac{487.5}{25 \times 10}$$

S = 0.39 J/g^oc. Ans.

EXERCISES

1. Choose the correct option:

(i) Ratio of linear, area, and volume expansion in solids is:

(a) 1:1:1
b) 1:2:3
(c) 1:2:1
(d) 3:2:1

Correct answer: (b) 1:2:3

(ii) Amongst object A and B, if the specific heat of object A is less than that of object B, then:

(a) Object A will get warm sooner
(b) Object B will get warm sooner
(c) Both will get warm at the same rate
(d) None of the above

Correct answer: (a) Object A will get warm sooner

(iii) Which one amongst the following is the best conductor of heat:

(a) Iron
(b) Asbestos
(c) Glass
(d) Wood

Correct answer: (a) Iron

(iv) In which one of the following heat cannot flow due to convection:

(a) Tea
(b) Water
(c) Wind
(d) Vacuum
Correct answer: (d) Vacuum

2. Fill in the blanks:
   (i) Heat is not matter; instead, it is energy.
   (ii) Temperature difference results in heat transfer.
   (iii) Heat transfer is possible in solids due to conduction.
   (iv) Medium is not required for heat transfer due to radiation.
   (v) Heat provided to change the physical state of matter results in a change in temperature; this process is called latent heat.

3) When two objects with different temperatures are put in contact with each other, they both achieve the same temperature after some time. Why is it so?

Ans-

When two objects with different temperatures are put in contact with each other, they both achieve the same temperature after some time due to the process of heat transfer known as thermal equilibrium.

Thermal equilibrium occurs as heat flows from the object with higher temperature to the object with lower temperature until both objects reach a common temperature.

This happens because the molecules in both objects interact and exchange energy until their average kinetic energy, which determines temperature, becomes equal.

4) What is latent heat?

Ans:- Latent heat is the amount of energy absorbed or released by a substance during a phase change, such as melting, freezing, boiling, or condensing, without a change in temperature.
For example:
Latent heat of fusion is the energy required to change a solid into a liquid at its melting point.
Latent heat of vaporization is the energy needed to convert a liquid into a gas at its boiling point.

5) Balloon filled with gas bursts when we take it close to fire, why?

Ans:- The balloon filled with gas bursts when taken close to fire due to the rapid expansion of the gas inside the balloon. The heat from the fire causes the gas molecules to move faster and spread out, increasing the pressure inside the balloon until it can no longer contain the expanding gas. This leads to the balloon bursting as a result of the increased pressure.

6) Convert the temperatures given below into given units (i) 14° F into Celsius. (ii) 100° C into Fahrenheit. (iii) 12 K into Celsius.

Ans:- (i) 14°F into Celsius:

To convert Fahrenheit to Celsius, we use the formula C = 5/9 (F - 32).

: C = 5/9 (14 - 32)

= 5/9 * (-18)

= -10°C. Therefore,

14°F is equal to -10°C.

(ii) 100°C into Fahrenheit:

To convert Celsius to Fahrenheit, we use the formula

F = 9/5 * C + 32.

: F = 9/5 * 100 + 32

= 180 + 32

= 212°F.

Therefore, 100°C is equal to 212°F.

(iii) To convert 12 K into Celsius, we use the formula:

C = K - 273.

Therefore,

12 K in Celsius

12 - 273 = -261°C.

7) Write three uses of specific heat of water in daily life.?

Ans:- Regulating Body Temperature: Water's high specific heat capacity helps regulate body temperature by absorbing heat during hot weather and releasing it slowly to keep the body cool.

Cooking Food: Specific heat of water allows it to heat up evenly and retain heat, making it ideal for cooking food as it ensures consistent temperature throughout the cooking process.

Heating Systems: Water's specific heat capacity is utilized in heating systems like radiators where water absorbs heat and circulates it to warm up buildings efficiently.

8) QS. The temperature of 1kg water is 600C. It is mixed with 1 kg water at 40 ^{o}c, then what will be the temperature of mixture?

Sol. Given, m_l = 1 kg; t_i= 60^{0}C; m_2= 1 kg; t_2 = 400C.

Let temperature of mixture be - t ^{o}C.

Specific heat of water = S (in both the cases)

Heat lost = Heat gained

m_1. S. (60 -t) = m_2S. (t -40)

Ix (60 - t) = 1 x (t - 40)

60 +40 = t + t

2t = 100

t = 50 ^{o}C

Therefore, temperature of mixture will be 500C.

Q. 9. The mass of a Copper vessel is 500 gm. Calculate heat required to raise its temperature by 400C. (Specific heat of copper is 0009 J/kg^{O}C)

Sol.: -

Given, Mass m = 500 gm = ½ kg

Specific heat S = 0•09 J/kg ^{o}c

Temp. difference Δt = 40 ^{o}c

Heat required = ms Δt = ½ × 0.09 × 40

= 1.80 joules.Ans.

10) .Length of an aluminium wire is 100 cm, what will be the increase in its length when its temperature is increased to 50°C from 30°C? Coefficient of linear expansion for aluminium is 26×10^{-6}/°C.

ans:-

The increase in length of an aluminium wire when its temperature is increased from 30°C to 50°C can be calculated using the formula:
Increase in length = coefficient of linear expansion × (initial length × increase in temperature)
Given that the initial length is 100 cm, and the coefficient of linear expansion for aluminium is 26×10^{-6}/°C, we can substitute the values to find the increase in length.

Therefore, the increase in length of the aluminium wire would be:
Increase in length = 26×10^{-6} × (100 cm × 20°C)
Increase in length = 26×10^{-6} × 200 cm
Increase in length = 0.0052 cm

Hence, the increase in length of the aluminium wire would be 0.0052 cm when its temperature is increased from 30°C to 50°C.

11) Define specific heat capacity?

ans:-

Specific heat capacity is the amount of heat required to raise the temperature of one unit of a substance by one degree. It is expressed in Joules per kilogram per degree Celsius (J/kg°C). Substances with higher specific heat capacity take longer to heat up and cool down, while those with lower specific heat capacity heat up and cool down more quickly.

12) What are the types of heat transfer? Write about them?

ans:-

Conduction: Heat transfer through conduction occurs in solids where heat energy is passed from one molecule to another without the actual movement of molecules. It depends on the nature of the substance and is also known as heat conductivity.

Convection: Convection involves the transfer of heat in liquids and gases. It occurs through the movement of fluids where warmer, lighter fluids rise, and cooler, denser fluids sink, creating convection currents.

Radiation: Heat transfer through radiation does not require a material medium and can occur in vacuum. Heat travels in straight lines and is transferred through radiations, similar to light energy.

13) Give few examples of effects of heat seen in our daily life.

ANS:-

Expansion of Substances: When objects are heated, they expand due to the increase in temperature. This expansion can lead to changes in the state of substances.

- Heat expansion in a solid substance-
  - linear expansion
  - superficial expansion
  - volumetric expansion
- Heat Expansion in Liquids
- Heat Expansion in gases

Temperature Variations: Different materials absorb and emit heat differently based on their temperature and surface characteristics. For example, a black-painted utensil absorbs more heat than a shiny steel utensil when exposed to sunlight.

The quantity of heat (Q) absorbed and emitted by an object depends on the following

1. On the mass of substance $Q \alpha m$ ....(1)

2. On the change of temperature $Q \alpha \Delta T$ ....(2)

3. On the nature of the material Hence, $Q \alpha m. \Delta T$ $Q = m.S. \Delta T$

Chapter -4

Internal question: (page -54)

1.What was the basis of classification of elements as done by Lothar Meyer?
Ans: - Meyer was working on classification of elements on the basis of atomic weights and atomic volumes.
2.Write the names and symbols of the first four elements found in groups I and II of Mendeleev's periodic table?
Ans:- group – 1 (Hydrogen, Lithium, Sodium, Potassium)
group –2 (Beryllium, Magnesium, Calcium, Strontium)

3.Some spaces were left empty in Mendeleev's periodic table. Write the names of the elements that were later placed in these gaps.
Ans:- endeléev left some gaps in his Periodic Table. Instead of looking upon these gaps as defects, he predicted the existence of some elements that had not been discovered at that time. Mendeléev named them by prefixing "Eka" to the name of preceding element in the same group scandium, gallium and germanium, discovered later, were called Eka-boron, Eka-aluminium and Eka-silicon, respectively.

4. Name the two elements whose atomic weights were corrected by Mendeleev.
Ans:- the atomic weights of the elements indium, euronium etc. were corrected
5.Why were inert gases placed in a separate group? Write the reasons
Ans:- Inert gases such as helium, neon and argon had not been discovered during Mendeleev's times so no space was kept in the periodic table for them. When they were discovered, they were placed in a separate column which was added to the periodic table as the zero group.

Internal question:- (page- 57)

1.According to the modern periodic table, the properties of an element are a periodic function of what?
Ans:- Ans. Periodic function of atomic number.

2. What is the number of elements in the second period?
Ans. 8 elements are in the second period.
3. Can you provide appropriate position to the isotopes of various elements in the periodic table? Clarify.
Ans. Appropriate position cannot be provided to the isotopes of various elements because their atomic number is not similar. But, in the modem periodic table isotopes of an element occupy only one position because their atomic number is same.
How are the position of Argon and Potassium determined in the Modern Periodic table?
Ans. On the basis of atomic number of elements.

4.Atomic number of three elements x, y and z are 6, 10 and 18 respectively, then state that:

- Which two elements are of the same group?
  Ans. y and z.
- Which two elements are of the same period?
  Ans. x and y.

Internal question _ (page 58)

1. How can you calculate the valency of an element by its electronic configuration?
Ans. The number of electrons present in the last shell of an element is its valency.
Like: Carbon $_6C = 1s^2, 2s^2\ 2p^2$, or 2, 4.
There are four electrons in the last shell of carbon, thus its valency will be four.

2.How does valency change on moving from top to bottom in a group ?
Ans. There is no change in the valency of elements on moving from top to bottom in a group.

Internal question -(page 60)

1.How does Ionisation energy change in a group?
Ans. On moving from top to bottom in a group, ionisation energy decreases because of gradual change in atomic size.
2. How does ionisation energy of elements of the same period change? Explain its reason.
Ans:- Lithium (Li) and Beryllium are placed in the same period, but ionisation energy of lithium is less than beryllium, because its Size is bigger and its last shell is not completely filled. It can be justified by the electronic configuration.
Li → 2,1
Be → 2,2
Thus, ionisation energy of Be is more than Lithium.

Internal -(page -61)

1.How does electron affinity differ from electronegativity?
Ans:- Electron affinity and electronegativity are different from each other. Electronegativity is the property of an atom to attract the shared electron pair in a covalent bond with another atom towards itself. Therefore, it is a relative quantity which does not have a unit whereas electron affinity is the energy released when an electron is added to an isolated gaseous atom and its unit is eV.
2.The elements of which group have the highest electron affinities?
Ans.: - 17th group

EXERCISE QUESTION: -

2) The physical and chemical properties of elements belonging to the same group are similar, why?

Ans. Physical and chemical properties of elements of a group are same, because:

Their electronic configuration is same.

Valency is same.

Properties of their oxides are same.

All the elements form same type of hydrides.

3) In which group and which period should hydrogen be placed? Comment.

Ans. Hydrogen is known as a rogue element, because of its tendency to form both anion as well as cation (H+) due to which it shows similarity in physical and chemical properties with group 17 and group 1. But it is suitable to place hydrogen in group I because its chemical properties resemble with elements of group I (Li, Na, K Rb and Cs).

4) Among the following pairs, select the element which has a bigger size and state the cause:

Mg (Atomic number 12) or Cl (Atomic number 17).

Ans. Atomic radius of Mg is bigger as on moving from left to right in a period atomic radius decreases.

Na (Atomic number 11) or K (Atomic number 19).

Ans. Size of Potassium will be bigger as on moving from top to bottom in a group atomic size of elements increases.

5) Atomic number of three elements A, B and C are 3, 9 and 11. Discuss with reason, that the chemical properties of which two elements are alike.

Ans.

element	Group	Period	Chemical Properties
Boron	13	2	Metalloid, forms compounds like BCl_3, Lewis acid.
Nitrogen	15	2	Non-metal, forms compounds like NH_3, Lewis base.
Neon	18	2	Noble gas, inert, full valence shell.

So, to answer the question: Boron (A) and Nitrogen (B) are the two elements whose chemical properties are more alike, although they still differ significantly due to their different groups. Top of Form Bottom of Form

Q. 6. Atomic number of three elements are 5, 7, and 10. State:

(i) Which element is of group 18?

Ans:- Element of atomic number 10 (Ne).Which element is of group 15 ?
Ans. Element of atomic number 7 (N).
(ii)Which element is of group of 13?
Ans. Element of atomic number 5 (B).
(iii)All these elements are of which period?
Ans. All these elements are of second period.

Q. 7. Among the three elements A, B and C in a triad, atomic number of A is 7 and atomic number of C is 39, then according to Dobereigners triad what will be the atomic mass of B?

Ans. Atomic mass of element B will be 23.

8) A part of periodic table is given as: Na, Mg ....
(i) How does the metallic character of the elements change?
Ans:- Metallic property of element decreases
How does electronegativity change?
Ans:- Electronegativity increases.
How does electron affinity change?
Ans:- Ionisation energy increases, but ionisation energy of Be is more than B (Boron) and of N (Nitrogen) is more than O (Oxygen) (Exceptional concept).

9.) Why did Mendeleev leave blank space in his periodic table? Discuss your answer with an example.
Ans. Mendeleev left some blank space in his periodic table. Mendeleev did not consider these blank spaces as defects. Some such elements discovered were named by using the prefix 'Eka'.
Later, the elements were discovered and EkaBoron, Eka-Aluminium and Eka-Silicon were named as Scandium, Gallium and Germanium.
10) Are Döbereiner's triads seen in Newlands' octets? Compare and write.
Ans:- yes, one triad can be seen in lewlands table.
Comparison:
Purpose: Both Döbereiner's triads and Newlands' octaves aimed to find a pattern in the properties of elements based on their atomic weights.
Structure: Döbereiner's triads grouped elements in sets of three, while Newlands' octaves organized them in a linear fashion, with every eighth element showing similar properties.
Limitations: Both systems had limitations in terms of the number of elements they could accommodate and the consistency of the patterns they observed. Döbereiner's triads could not group all elements, and Newlands' octaves worked well only for lighter elements.

11) . In the modern periodic table, how do the following properties change on moving from top to bottom in a period?

Valency, (ii) Atomic size, (iii) Ionisation potential, (iv) Electronegativity.
Ans.
(i) Valency : On moving from top to bottom in a group, valency of elements is same, but on moving from left to right in a period valency first increases from 1 to 4 and then decreases to 0.

Atomic size: On moving from top to bottom in a group the atomic size increases due tothe increase in the number of shells. But on moving from left to right in a period atomic size decreases due to increase in the nuclear charge.

Ionisation potential: On moving from top to bottom in a group ionisation potential decreases but on moving from left to right in a period ionisation potential increases. Like ionisation potential increases on moving from Li to Ne.

Electronegativity: On moving from top to bottom in a group, electronegativity decreases whereas on moving from left to right in a period, electronegativity increases.
(12) . Electronic configuration of an element B is 2, 8, 7 and it reacts with element A to form AB2 type of ionic compound. What will be the valency of element A ?
Ans. Name of the element B - The element with this electronic configuration is Chlorine (Cl).
Element B (Chlorine) reacts with Element A to form an AB_2 type of ionic compound.
This indicates that Element A has to balance the charges of two chlorine ions (Cl^-) to form a neutral compound.
Determining the Valency of Element A
To achieve electrical neutrality in the AB_2 compound:
Each Chlorine (Cl) ion has a charge of -1.
Two Chlorine ions will have a total charge of -2.
To balance this charge, Element A must have a +2 charge.
In ionic compounds, the valency of an element refers to its ability to combine with other elements to achieve a stable electronic configuration.
Therefore, Element A must have a valency of +2.

Q. 13. Compare the arrangement of elements in Modern periodic table and Mendeleev's periodic table.
Ans. Comparison between. arrangement of elements between Modern periodic table and Mendeleev's periodic table:
Modern periodic table: Modern periodic table is based on atomic number. Modern periodic table IS arranged on the bases of increasing atomic number. Position of each element is decided on the basis of its electronic configuration. It clearly signifies the periodicity in

properties of elements. 92 elements got position in this table, After atomic number 92 synthetic elements (up to atomic number 118) are placed in this table.
Mendeleev's periodic table: In Mendeleev's periodic table, only 63 elements were placed. According to Mendeleev's periodic law the physical and chemical properties of elements are a periodic function of their atomic mass.
In Mendeleev's periodic table: (i) Position of hydrogen is indefinite, (ii) Heavier elements are placed before lighter elements, (iii) Isotopes have not been given separate place. (iv) On moving from one element towards another atomic mass do not increase in a definite form.
This way, arrangement of elements in Modern periodic table and Mendeleev's periodic table are different.

Chapter -5

Q-1. Choose the right option.

(i) There are about 2234 insects, 56 birds and 3 snakes on a mango tree. The pyramid of energy would be

(a) Straight (b) Inverted (c) rectangular (d) uncertain

(ii) Fungi started growing on a moist piece of bread left in the open. After sometime some insects like house flies etc. were seen there. The organisms at the last trophic level would be-

(a) Food (b) bread (c) house fly (d) none

(iii) There are 3 stages in the life cycle of an insect - egg, larva, pupa, adult. If the stages of egg, larva and pupa are completed in the body of a particular organism then the insect's life cycle is completed in how many ecosystems?

(a) 1 (b) 2 (c) 3 (d) 4

(iv) What would happen if all insect eating birds were removed from a particular cropland area?

(a) Crop production will increase (b) Insect infestation will increase

(c) Increase in the number of other birds (d) No effect

(v) Cow feeds on grass. Its dung is used to make dung cakes which are used as fuel. The burning of the dung cakes produces smoke that reaches the atmosphere and the ashes are mixed with soil. This adds nutrients for grass to grow. This process is an example of-

(a) Food chain (b) Food web (c) Nutrient cycle (d) Life cycle

(vi) The food chain in a pond starts from some water plants that are eaten by certain fishes, those eaten by others extending finally to humans. The energy here from one trophic level to another will-

(a) Gradually decrease (b) gradually increase

(c) will be the same (d) will be less sometime and more sometime.

(vii) The number of organisms in a garden was estimated as 5567 grasses, 453 shrubs, 23 trees and 7769 animals. The primary productivity of this area will be nearly equal to-

(a) Biomass of all organisms of the garden (b) Biomass of all the plants of the garden (c) Biomass of the animals of the garden (d) Biomass of only 5567 grasses

(viii) In any food chain generally the first trophic levels are the _______ (producers)

Q-2. A type of fungi is grown on rice husk. We eat the fungi. Does it show a food chain? Illustrate the food chain. What is the source of energy for this food chain?

Ans-

Fungi is a decomposer which decomposes complex compounds into simpler substances. A type of fungi which is grown by humans on rice husk is mushroom Which we eat .it is a man-made ecosystem. It represents a simple food chain. Here the sun is the source of energy. Mushroom decomposes rice

Husk and produces food by converting radiation Into chemical energy and nourishes itself. Though it is a decomposer in other food chain but Here it is eaten by human which makes It a primary producer and human as the primary Consumers Food chain

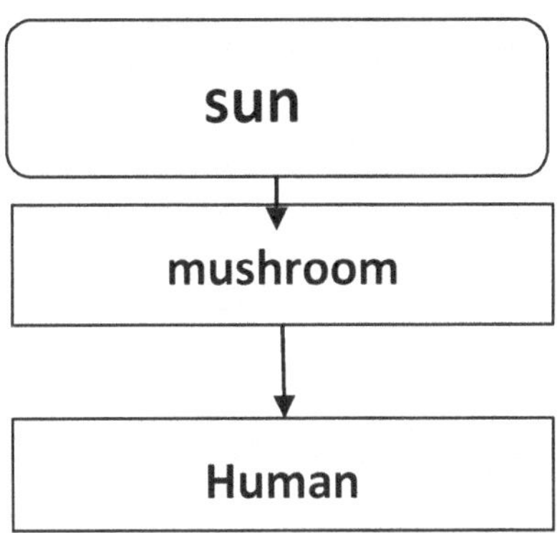

Q-3. How does energy flow in any ecosystem? Explain in your own words.

Ans-

Any food chain actually represents the pathway of flow of energy and It is very difficult to find out the amount of energy at each trophic level. We thus usually presume biomass as a basis to find out the energy at each trophic level.

Means if 1000 kg of plants (producers) are there they will provide energy only for 100 kg primary consumers. Which is $\frac{100}{1000} \times 100 = 10\%$ and so on.

As we can see in the energy flow pyramid Plants (producers) can convert nearly 1% of solar energy to that stored in bonds of chemical compounds synthesized by the process of photosynthesis. Of this only 10% (0.1% of solar energy) is available for organisms of the next trophic level. Only 10% of this again is converted to biomass at the second trophic level and available to those of the third trophic level. Thus efficiency of energy conversion at each trophic level is 10%. This law is known as 10% law.

. The flow of energy is unidirectional. The energy converted by plants cannot be converted back to solar energy.

Q-4)What will happen if only plants and humans are left on earth as living organisms or biotic component?

Ans-

As we know that more complex the food chain or web is the more balanced it becomes. But if only plants and humans are left on earth as living organism it will make a single food chain where plants are the producers and humans are primary consumer ,there will not be any secondary ,tertiary ,or decomposers. This will creat two major problems Which are as follows-

Unstable food chain: - when there is more food chain then it creates a stable ecosystem, where each organism is dependent on one another but in this case plants and humans will not be able create that stable ecosystem.
Incomplete energy cycle: - as there are no decomposers the energy that plants and humans will accumulate from sun it will net get recycled, which is very essential for plants and humans in the long run.

Q-5) What will happen if the natural flow of energy in an ecosystem is disrupted? Explain with an example.
Ans-
Any food chain actually represents the pathway of flow of energy. A food web shows several such pathways. It becomes clear from food chain and pyramid of energy, that the flow of energy is unidirectional.
if the natural flow of energy in an ecosystem is disrupted means food web is disrupted. Which means the stability of the ecosystem will get destroyed in ecosystem energy flows is in the form of heat.
Ex.-
If at any level producer or consumer Or decomposers are not present then The stable ecosystem will not function properly.

Q-6) How does the availability of energy affect the number of organisms at different trophic levels?
Ans-
Food chain (trophic level) of an eco-system based on the number of producers and primary, secondary and tertiary consumers is known as "Pyramid of number".
When we see an ecosystem on the basis of number, then in that trophic level number of producers will be maximum, then the number of first, second and third series of consumers goes on decreasing. 'Thus, in this trophic level an (upright) straight pyramid is formed. But if we consider a tree of a forest eco-system and form a Pyramid producer tree is minimum and in the first level, number consumer (bird) is more and Consumers of second level are maximum. It is represented by the help of bio number pyramid.
Ecological Pyramids: If we represent the various trophic levels of an eco-system in the ratio of number of organisms, biomass and amount of stored energy then a pyramid like

structure is obtained which is known as Ecological pyramid. Ecological pyramid is named on the basis of the factor based on its formation.

For example: In the Grassland ecosystem number of grass is maximum, then number of herbivorous organisms is less and number of carnivorous organisms of various trophic levels gradually go on decreasing. It is clear that more place will be given to grass (producers), then herbivores little less and for carnivores, place is to be gradually decreased. This way the pyramid formed will be known as Pyramid of number because it is based on the number of organism of various levels of the eco-system.

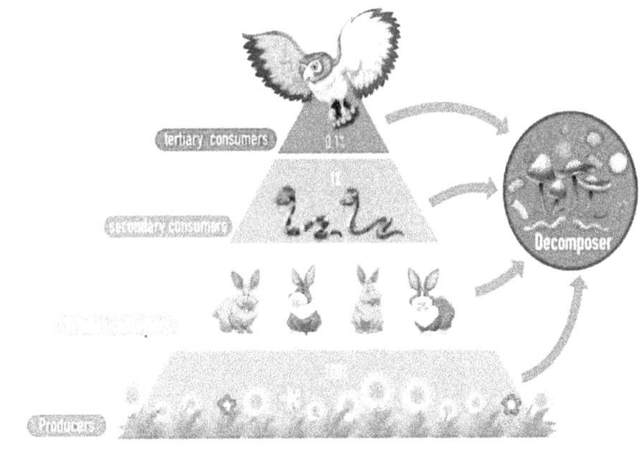

SIMPLIFIED ECOLOGICAL PYRAMID

Q-7) the effect of human beings on an ecosystem. Explain why you think so and suggest some means to minimize the same

Ans.: -

Human beings are the top of energy pyramid and also the increase in the number of the top consumer(humans)Is affecting adversely the ecosystem. To fulfil the needs of The human beings, many things have been done and still going on which are bad for the ecosystem like-

Uncontrolled hunting, fishing, deforestation etc.

Excessive use of pesticides, insecticides, chemical fertilizers etc.

Excessive pollution, industrialisation etc.

Chapter - 6

Multiple choice question: -

Here are the correct options:

(i) Which one of the options given below is a good conductor of electricity:

- (c) Copper wire

(ii) The instrument used to measure current in a circuit is:

- (b) Ammeter

(iii) The relation between V and I for a conducting wire is:

- (b) A fixed ratio

(iv) The resistance of an electrical instrument is 2.2 ohm and potential difference is 220 volt s. Find out the value of current on connecting the instrument to an electric source:

- (a) 5 A

(v) The equivalent resistance of the following diagram would be:

- (c) 10 Ω

(vi) The equivalent resistance of the following diagram would be–

- (b) 20 Ω

2. Fill in the blanks: -

(i) The potential difference of resistors connected in a series would be the sum of the indivi dual potential differences.

(ii) In resistors connected in a parallel combination, the current flowing across each resistor would be different, depending on the resistance of each resistor.

(iii) We show the consumption of electricity in Kwh or in joules.

(iv) The filament used in electric bulbs is made of tungsten metal.

(v) The resistance of a conductor increases with temperature.

4. What is a fuse and of what material is it made?

Ans:-

A fuse is a safety device used in electrical circuits to protect against excessive current flow, which can cause overheating and potential fires. It consists of a thin wire or strip of metal t hat melts and breaks the circuit when the current exceeds a certain level, thereby stopping t he flow of electricity.

Fuses are typically made of materials with low melting points, such as tin, lead, or an alloy of tin and lead. These materials ensure that the fuse will melt quickly when exposed to exce ssive current, effectively protecting the circuit and connected devices.

5.explain ohm's law with graph.

Ans:-

Ohm's law definition, The potential difference or voltage(V) across the ends of an Ohmic conductor is directly proportional to the current (I) flowing through the ohmic conductor, provided the physical condition remains constant or unchanged."

Here the physical condition means temperature, pressure, humidity, etc.

you can also define the Ohm law-

"Ohms law states that the current flowing in a conductor is directly proportional to the applied voltage across the ends of the conductor at constant physical condition."

That means, $V \propto I$ or $I \propto V$

$\therefore$ $V = RI$ or $I = V/R$

Or, $V = IR$ ....(1)

Where, V = Potential difference across the ends of conductor,

I = current flowing through the conductor

R = proportionality constant also known as Resistance of the circuit.

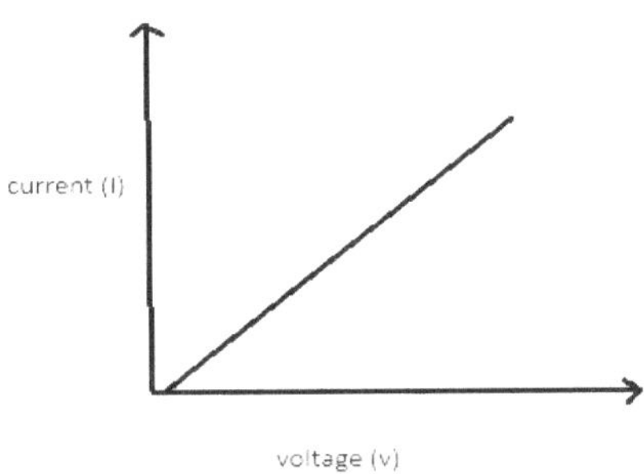

6.If an electric bulb consumes 2400 J energy in a minute, calculate the power of the bulb?

Ans:- Power is the rate at which energy is consumed. To calculate the power of the bulb we can use the formula

$$\text{Power} = \frac{Energy}{\text{Time}}$$

Given:

- Energy (E) = 2400 Joules
- Time (t) = 1 minute = 60 seconds

So, the power (P) of the bulb is:

$$P = \frac{2400\text{ J}}{60\text{ s}} = 40\text{ W}$$

The power of the bulb is 40 watts

7. An electric heater has 3 kw, 220 v, stamped on it. Find values of the following–

(a) Electric current

(b) Resistance of the heater

(c) Cost of electricity if unit cost is Rs. 1.50/kwh and heater is used for 10 hours

Ans:-

To find the electric current, we can use the formula:

Power = Voltage × Current

Given:

- Power (P) = 3 kW = 3000 W
- Voltage (V) = 220 V

Rearranging the formula to solve for current (I):

I = P/V

So,

I=3000 W /220 V ≈ 13.64 A

The electric current is approximately 13.64 amperes.

(b) Resistance of the heater

To find the resistance of the heater, we can use Ohm's Law, which states:

V=I×R

Rearranging the formula to solve for resistance (R):

$$R = \frac{V}{I}$$

Given:

- Voltage (V) = 220 V
- Current (I) ≈ 13.64 A (from the previous calculation)

So,

$$R = \frac{220\ V}{13.64\ A} \approx 16.13\ \Omega$$

The resistance of the heater is approximately 16.13 ohms

(c) Cost of electricity if unit cost is Rs. 1.50/kwh and heater is used for 10 hours

To calculate the cost of electricity, we can use the formula:

Cost =Power × Time × Rate

Given:

- Power (P) = 3 kW
- Time (t) = 10 hours
- Rate = Rs. 1.50/kWh

So,

Cost=3 kW×10 hours×1.50 Rs/kWh=45 Rs

The cost of electricity for using the heater for 10 hours is Rs. 45.

8. (i) Why are domestic circuits not arranged in a series combination?

(ii) Why is only tungsten metal used to make filaments of bulbs?

Ans:-

(i) Domestic circuits are not arranged in a series combination because if one appliance fails or is turned off, the entire circuit would be interrupted, causing all appliances to stop working. Additionally, in a series circuit, the voltage is divided among the appliances, whic h means each appliance would receive less voltage and may not function properly.

(ii) Tungsten is used to make filaments of bulbs because it has a very high melting point (ar ound 3422°C) and can withstand high temperatures without melting. This allows the filame nt to glow brightly without burning out quickly. Tungsten also has good electrical conducti vity, making it an ideal material for light bulb filaments.

9. If a current of 0.5 A flows for 20 minutes in a filament of a bulb, then what would be the quantity of electrical charge flowing in the circuit?
Ans:-To find the quantity of electrical charge flowing in the circuit, we can use the formula:

$$Q = I \times t$$

Where:

- Q is the charge in coulombs (C)
- I is the current in amperes (A)
- t is the time in seconds (s)

Given:

- Current (I) = 0.5 A
- Time (t) = 20 minutes = 20 × times 60 seconds = 1200 seconds

So,
Q = 0.5 A × 1200 s =600 C
The quantity of electrical charge flowing in the circuit is 600 coulombs.

10. In a house, 4 electric bulbs of 40 watt burn for 5 hours, 2 bulbs of 60 watts for 6 hours and 3 fans of 80 watts run for 6 hours, daily. What would be the cost of electricity, for one month of that home, if the rate is 50 paise per unit?
Ans:-
Let's break it down step by step:

1. Calculate the daily energy consumption:
    - 4 bulbs of 40 W for 5 hours: 4 × 40 W × 5 hours = 800 Wh
    - 2 bulbs of 60 W for 6 hours: 2×60 W×6 hours = 720 Wh
    - 3 fans of 80 W for 6 hours: 3×80 W×6 hours = 1440 Wh
2. Total daily energy consumption:
   800 Wh+720 Wh+1440 Wh = 2960 Wh = 2.96 kWh
3. Calculate the monthly energy consumption:
   2.96 kWh/day×30 days = 88.8 kWh
4. Calculate the cost of electricity:
    - Rate = 50 paise per unit (1 unit = 1 kWh)

   88.8 kWh × 0.50 Rs/kWh = 44.4Rs

The cost of electricity for one month would be Rs. 44.4.

11. Discuss the following questions –

(i) What would be the effect on the circuit if one bulb out of three bulbs arranged in a series combination becomes fused?

(ii) What would be the effect if one bulb out of three arranged in parallel combination malfunctions?

Ans:-

(i) In a series combination, if one bulb out of three becomes fused, the entire circuit will be interrupted. This is because the current flows through each bulb in sequence, and a break i n any part of the circuit will stop the flow of electricity. As a result, all the bulbs will go out.

(ii) In a parallel combination, if one bulb out of three malfunctions, the other bulbs will con tinue to work. This is because each bulb has its own separate path to the power source. The current can still flow through the other paths, so the remaining bulbs will remain lit. This is one of the advantages of parallel circuits in domestic wiring.

13. If the potential difference generated by a battery across a circuit of two bulbs, combined in series, is 6 volts, and the potential difference at the first bulb is 2 volts, find out the potential difference at the second bulb?

Ans:-

In a series circuit, the total potential difference (voltage) across the circuit is the sum of the potential differences across each component. Given that the total potential difference is 6 vo lts and the potential difference at the first bulb is 2 volts, we can find the potential differenc e at the second bulb by subtracting the potential difference at the first bulb from the total p otential difference:

$V_{total} = V_1 + V_2$

Given:

- $V_{total} = 6$ V
- $V_1 = 2$ V

So,

$$V_2 = V_{total} - V_1 = 6\text{ V} - 2\text{ V} = 4\text{ V}$$

The potential difference at the second bulb is 4 volts.

15. 9 volt battery is arranged in series combination with resistors of 2Ω, 3Ω, 4Ω, 5Ω and 12Ω, what would be the current flowing across the 2Ω resistor?

Ans:-

In a series circuit, the current flowing through each resistor is the same. To find the current , we first need to calculate the total resistance of the circuit and then use Ohm's Law.

1. Calculate the total resistance:

$R_{total} = 2\Omega+3\Omega+4\Omega+5\Omega+12\Omega = 26\Omega$

2. Use Ohm's Law to find the current:

$I = V/R_{total}$

Given:

- Voltage (V) = 9 V
- Total resistance (R_{total}) = 26 Ω

So,

$I = 9\ V /26\ \Omega \approx 0.346\ A$

The current flowing across the 2Ω resistor is approximately 0.346 amperes.

17. On a bulb, 200 V - 100 W is printed. What would be the resistance of the bulb? If 5 of these bulbs burn for 4 hours, what would be the amount of electricity consumed and the cost of electricity, if the rate is 50 paise per unit?

Ans:-

Let's break it down step by step:

1. Calculate the resistance of the bulb: Using the formula $P=V^2R$, we can rearrange it to solve for resistance R:

$$R = \frac{V^2}{P}$$

Given:

- Voltage (V) = 200 V
- Power (P) = 100 W

So,

$$R=\frac{200^2 V^2}{100\ w} = \frac{40000\ V^2}{100\ W} = 400\Omega$$

The resistance of the bulb is 400 ohms.

2. Calculate the amount of electricity consumed:
   - Power of one bulb = 100 W
   - Number of bulbs = 5
   - Time = 4 hours

Total power consumption:

Total Power=5×100 W=500 W=0.5 kW

Total energy consumed:

Energy=Power×Time=0.5 kW×4 hours=2 kWh

3. Calculate the cost of electricity:

    - Rate = 50 paise per unit (1 unit = 1 kWh)

Cost=2 kWh×0.50 Rs/kWh=1 Rs

The cost of electricity for burning 5 bulbs for 4 hours is Rs. 1.

Chapter -7

1) Multiple choice question: -

1. The internal wall of the stomach is usually not injured by HCl because of:
   - (b) mucous
2. Gaseous exchange occurs during respiration between:
   - (b) alveoli of lungs and surrounding capillaries
3. Oxygenated blood flows from lungs to heart by:
   - (b) pulmonary vein
4. Kidney is composed of several:
   - (a) nephron

2)How is a vein different from an artery?

Arteries	Veins
Arteries carry blood from the heart to the tissues. Arteries carry pure blood except pulmonary artery which carries impure blood. Blood flows with jerks in it. Blood pressure is high. Its walls are thick and elastic. After the death of the organism it becomes empty. It is deeply situated in the body.	Veins carry blood from the tissues to the heart. Veins carry impure blood except pulmonary vein which carries pure blood. In veins, pressure of blood is less and blood flows slowly. Their walls are thin and less elastic. After the death of organism blood remains in it. It lies near the upper surface.

3) Differentiate between respiration in the presence and absence of oxygen.

Ans:-

Aerobic respiration	Anaerobic respiration
This process occurs in the presence of oxygen (O_2). It gets completed in the cytoplasm and	It occurs in the absence of O_2. It gets completed only in the cytoplasm.

mitochondria of the cell. In this process glucose is completely oxidized. By the complete oxidation of one molecule of glucose 673kcal (2813kJ) energy is released. In this process, one molecule of glucose releases 38 ATP molecules.	In this, incomplete oxidation of glucose takes place and at the end CO2 and alcohol are formed. By the incomplete oxidation of one molecule of glucose 21kcal (88 kJ) energy is released. In this process, one molecule of glucose releases 2 ATP molecules.

4.. What are the differences between the sources of energy of producers and consumer? Clarify this.

Ans:-

Producer's Energy Sources (Green Plants)	Consumer Energy Sources
Producer (plants) absorbs mineral substances and water from the soil. Plants themselves prepare organic substances. In this reaction, carbon dioxide, water, chlorophyll and sunlight are required. This process of preparation of food by producers (plants) is called photosynthesis. In this process oxygen gas (O2) is released. Energy source of producers (plants) is the process of photosynthesis.	Consumers (animals) require food or organic substances for their survival For the physical growth and repair in every cell of the body, carbohydrate, fats and proteins is continuously required. "Such substances which release energy after hydrolysis and are helpful for growth, development and repair of tissues of the body are known as food. Energy source of consumers (animals) is food.

5) What is the mutual relationship of animals and plants on the basis of food?

Ans:-

Like all organisms, green plants also require food. Plants absorb mineral salts and water from the soil. Plants prepare organic substances themselves. In this process carbon dioxide (CO_2), water (H_2O), chlorophyll and sunlight is required. All the organisms require and release carbon-dioxide (CO_2), which is used by green plants to prepare their food by photosynthesis. All the organisms depend directly or indirectly on plants or on other organisms which depend on plants. Process of photosynthesis is a fundamental link of bio food chain. This way, plants and animals are related to each other for food.

6) Why is formation of urine and its removal necessary for humans?

Ans:-

Waste products are produced as a result of metabolic activities in the body of all organisms which are known as excretory products. By the decomposition of carbohydrate and fats, carbon dioxide and water are formed. By the decomposition of proteins ammonia, urea and uric acid are formed which is known as urine. Thus, to maintain balance in body activities of all organisms, formation of these excretory products (urine) and their removal from the body is necessary.

7) What is the difference between substances transported by xylem and phloem?

Ans:-

Xylem	Phloem
In plants, the products transported in xylem are water and mineral salts. Vessels and tracheid's of xylem combine and transport water and mineral salts. Pores of roots are in contact with the soil which absorbs water and mineral salts in the form of ions. Substance flow against gravity	In plants, food and other products are transported by phloem. By the sieve tubes of phloem, photosynthetic products are transported towards the roots, fruits and the regions of growth. Transportation in phloem takes place on both the sides. It goes both ways.

8) What is the function of HCl secreted in the stomach?

Ans:-

Stomach is a bag like structure in alimentary canal. Mainly it receives the masticated food and it secretes gastric juices from gastric glands. In this gastric juices hcl is also secreted, which mainly destroys any kind of harmful bacteria germs, and other thing.

11) Explain how blood flows in two pathways from the heart?

Ans:-

Blood flows through two pathways simultaneously from the heart. That is in one pathway de-oxygenated blood from heart is oxygenated via lungs and returned to it. While in the other oxygenated blood is deoxygenated via all parts of the body (including the lungs) and returned to heart.

HEART AND LUNGS BLOOD FLOW

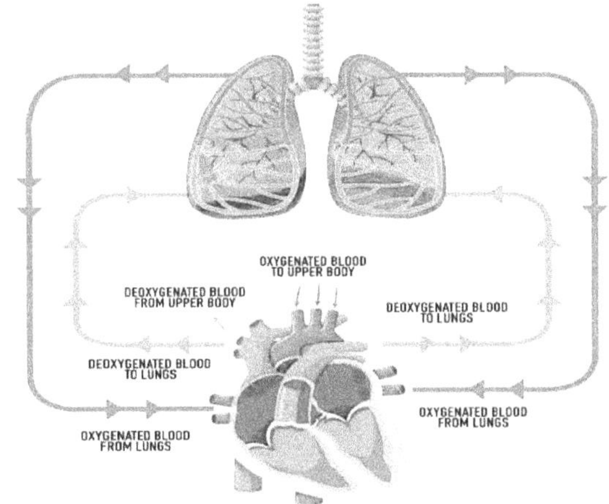

The two pathways are shown in Figure we can trace these pathways from the heart. As the left ventricle contracts oxygenated blood flows out into the large artery called aorta that divides into several arteries carrying blood to the tissues.
Capillaries thereafter carry blood to the cells and carry deoxygenated blood back to veins that collectively carry back blood to the right auricle of heart. This is one pathway.

The other starts with contraction of right ventricle as deoxygenated blood flows out through pulmonary arteries to the lungs. There arteries and capillaries carry blood to sites of gaseous exchange from where oxygenated blood is returned via capillaries to veins to the pulmonary vein that carry blood to the left auricle of heart.

Extra question:-

Q-1) makes a clear diagram of human digestive system. Explain its working.

Or

make diagram of digestive system and describe organs.

Ans:-

The digestive tract of humans starts with the mouth and ends with the anus. It includes different structures such as the mouth, oesophagus, pancreas, stomach, small intestine, large intestine, liver, gall bladder, and anus.

Flow chart:-

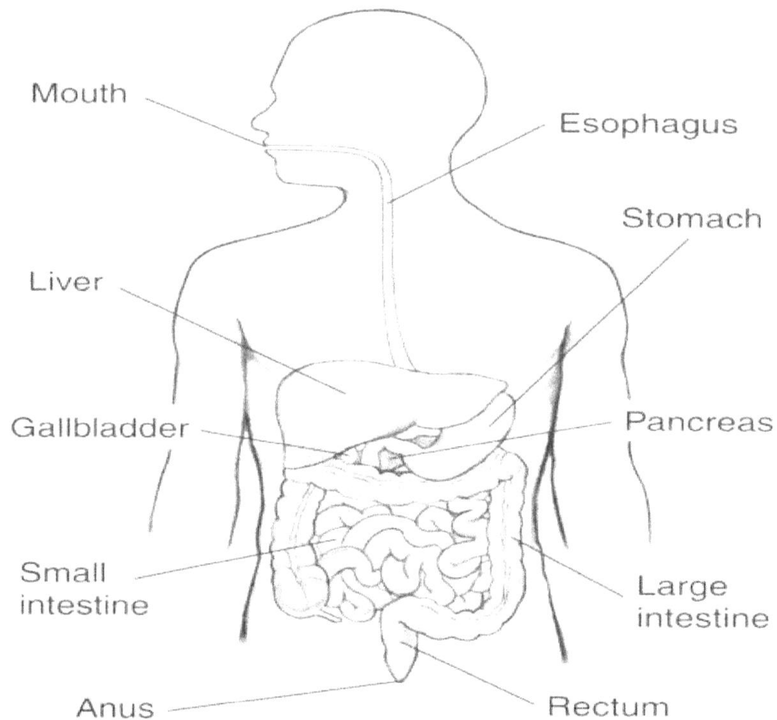

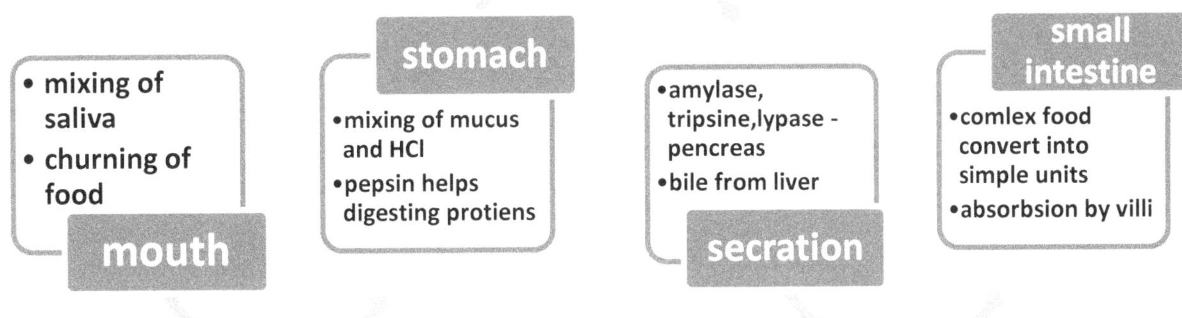

Ingestion:

The very first step involves mastication (chewing). The salivary glands, along with the tongue, help to moisten and lubricate food, before being pushed down into the food pipe.

Mixing and Movement:

It involves the process of lubricating and manipulating food and pushing it down the food through the food pipe (using peristalsis), and into the stomach.

Secretion:

The stomach, small intestine, liver, and pancreas secrete enzymes and acids to aid the process of digestion. It functions by breaking down food particles into simple components and easily absorbable components.

Digestion:

The process of converting complex food particles into simpler substances in the presence of enzymes and acids secreted by different digestive organs.

Absorption:

This process begins in the small intestine where most of the nutrients and minerals are absorbed by finger like structure called villi. The excess water in the indigestible matter is absorbed by the large intestines.

Excretion:

The process of removing indigestible substances and waste by-products from the body through the process of defecation.

Q-2) make a diagram of human respiratory system and explain its working.

Ans:-

In our cells where food is oxidised and energy is released, this process called as respiration. The respiratory tract in humans is made up of the following parts:

External nostrils – For the intake of air.

Nasal chamber – which is lined with hair and mucus to filter the air from dust and dirt.

Pharynx – It is a passage behind the nasal chamber and serves as the common passageway for both air and food.

Larynx – Known as the soundbox as it houses the vocal chords, which are paramount in the generation of sound.

Trachea – It is a long tube passing through the mid-thoracic cavity.

Bronchi – The trachea divides into left and right bronchi.

Bronchioles – Each bronchus is further divided into finer channels known as bronchioles.

Alveoli – The bronchioles terminate in balloon-like structures known as the alveoli.

Lungs – Humans have a pair of lungs, which are sac-like structures and covered by a double-layered membrane known as pleura.

Inhalation and Exhalation

The respiratory system helps in breathing (also known as pulmonary ventilation.) The air inhaled through the nose moves through the pharynx, larynx, trachea and into the lungs. The air is exhaled back through the same pathway. Changes in the volume and pressure in the lungs aid in pulmonary ventilation.

Exchange of Gases between Lungs and Bloodstream

Inside the lungs, the oxygen and carbon dioxide enter and exit respectively through millions of microscopic sacs called alveoli. The inhaled oxygen diffuses into the pulmonary capillaries, binds to haemoglobin and is pumped through the bloodstream. The carbon dioxide from the blood diffuses into the alveoli and is expelled through exhalation.

Exchange of Gases between Bloodstream and Body Tissues

The blood carries the oxygen from the lungs around the body and releases the oxygen when it reaches the capillaries. The oxygen is diffused through the capillary walls into the body tissues. The carbon dioxide also diffuses into the blood and is carried back to the lungs for release.

Energy release in cell:-

Oxidation of glucose releases a large amount of energy.

Glucose → Pyruvate → CO_2 + H_2O + Energy

3) Human excretory system and describe about its parts.

Ans

Human excretory system: In humans, the excretory system consists of a pair of kidneys, a pair of ureters, urinary bladder and urethra.

Kidneys are two bean shaped organs lying at the back of the abdomen, one on either side of the vertebral column. Waste products from the blood and urine are removed by the kidney.

A Nephron is the basic filtration unit of the kidney. It is a cluster of thin walled blood capillaries.

The urine produced by filtering the blood is transported to the urinary bladder. This is done by a pair of ureters. Ureters are long muscular tubes.

Urinary bladder is a muscular bag like structure which can hold urine. The urinary bladder is under the control of nerves. When the bladder is full one get urge to urinate.

This urine is thrown out of the body through urethra.

Apart from the kidney, the skin and lungs are also helpful in the excretion.

4) Make a clear diagram of nephron and explain working?

Ans:-

Each of your kidneys is made up of about a million filtering units called nephrons. Each nephron includes a filter, called the glomerulus, and a tubule. The nephrons work through a two-step process: the glomerulus filters your blood, and the tubule returns needed substances to your blood and removes wastes. The glomerulus filters your blood as blood flows into each nephron, it enters a cluster of tiny blood vessels—the glomerulus. The thin walls of the glomerulus allow smaller molecules, wastes, and fluid—mostly water—to pass into the tubule. Larger molecules, such as proteins and blood cells, stay in the blood vessel. The tubule returns needed substances to your blood and removes wastes

A blood vessel runs alongside the tubule. As the filtered fluid moves along the tubule, the blood vessel reabsorbs almost all of the water, along with minerals and nutrients your body needs in henle's loop. The tubule helps remove excess acid from the blood. The remaining fluid and wastes in the tubule become urine.

Q-5) labelled diagram of heart and working of it.

Ans:-

Heart:

The heart is the vital organ of the human body and is responsible for transportation in our body.

The heart comprises four chambers: two auricles (upper chambers), two ventricles (lower chambers)

A muscular wall known as the septum separates the two sides of the heart.

Function:

The heart's primary function is to pump blood throughout the body.

It supplies oxygen and nutrients to the tissues and removes carbon dioxide and waste from the blood.

It also helps to maintain adequate blood pressure throughout the body.

Heart pumps the blood throughout the body, hence playing an important role in maintaining body temperature.

Blood flow in the heart:

The arteries receive oxygenated blood from the heart and supply it throughout the body. Whereas, the veins carry the deoxygenated blood from all the body parts to the heart for oxygenation.

The right atrium receives blood from the veins and pumps it to the right ventricle.

The right ventricle pumps the blood received from the right atrium to the lungs.

The left atrium receives oxygenated blood from the lungs and pumps it to the left ventricle.

The left ventricle pumps the oxygenated blood throughout the body.

Chapter -8

Exercise .

Choose the right option-

(i) Which of the following is a plant hormone?

(a) Insulin (b) Thyroxine (c) Estrogen (d) Cytokinin

(ii) this is not a part of the structure of a nerve cell-

(a) dendrite (b) nucleus (c) axon (d) cellulosic cell wall

(iii) A gland present in our brain that controls hormonal secretions of several other glands in our body.

(a) Pituitary (b) liver (c) adrenal (d) pineal

(iv) A hormone from this gland controls the level of sugar in blood-

(a) Parathyroid (b) Pancreas (c) Adrenal (d) Pineal

(v) When we asleep at night and are bit by a mosquito, we often try to kill the mosquito. This action is controlled by-

(a) Pituitary gland (b) spinal cord and brain (c) hormones (d) pineal gland

2. Make schematic line diagrams and describe a reflex action of our body.

Ans-

i)when our hand touches a hot utensil it instantly moves away from it. The stimulus of heat passes to our hands through the cells that are in direct contact to the stimulus.

ii)They are then carried forward by nerves called as sensory nerves to the spinal cord and further to the brain.

iii)A response is effected against the stimulus from spinal cord or brain through nerves called as motor neurons.

iv)These influence the muscles of our arms in such a way that contraction and relaxation movements occur, eventually leading to the movement of our hand away from the hot utensil.

The complete circuit from sensing a stimulus to effecting a response is called as a reflex action.

3. Write a note on the role of spinal cord and brain on reflex action.
Ans-
Reflex actions are quick reactions. It's an unintentional activity that doesn't require any thought. When we touch a hot object, for example, we instinctively remove our hands without thinking.
Role of spinal cord; - reflex actions are controlled by spinal cord with the sensory nerves and motor nerves.
Role of brain: - reflex action is not controlled by brain, it just registers the action after some time.

4. 'There is a coordination between the secretion of hormones and the nervous system', justify the statement.
Ans-
A connection between nervous system and glands that release hormones exists all through our body. This connection and co-ordination is important for us to function. Nervous system passes signals that start the secretion of hormones and also passes the signal to stop the secretion of hormone. This co-ordination could be understood by following
ex.-
a hormone of pituitary gland controls the secretion of thyroxin from thyroid. If thyroxin level increases in blood a signal is passed by the nervous system, then the release of the pituitary hormone stops which stops the secretion of thyroxin from thyroid.

5. Illustrate a nerve cell with a neat and labelled drawing and describe it.
Ans-

The structure of neuron: Nerve cells or neurons are the structural and functional units of the nervous system. It consists of three major parts namely, -
(i)Cell body (ii)dendrites (iii) Axon.
Cell Body: It is irregular in shape or polyhedral. The cell body contains cytoplasm and certain granular bodies called Nissles granules which contain a group of ribosomes for protein synthesis.
ii)Dendrites: Dendrites are short fibres which branch repeatedly and protrude out of the cell body. They transmit electrical impulse towards the cyton.
iii)Axon: They are long fibres arising from the cell body with the branched distal end.
It terminates in bulb-like structures called synaptic knob. It is filled with chemicals called neurotransmitters.

6. How are involuntary actions controlled in our body, explain with a diagram?
Ans-
Actions which occur before thinking or information of stimulation known to brain is called involuntary action. These actions are performed and controlled by spinal cord.
Ex.- sneezing, blinking, are reflex or involuntary action.
Flow diagram: -
Stimulation → receptor organ → sensory nerve → spinal chor →motor nerve →action by muscles

7. Write an example of chemical control in plants.
Ans-
Chemical coordination in plants:
Plant hormones released by plants, aid in chemical coordination in plants. Plant hormones include auxin, cytokinin, gibberellin, and abscisic acid. These hormones control how the plants grow and develop. They control several plant metabolic processes. These hormones respond to environmental factors such as temperature and light.
Ex.- 1) cytokinin is in charge of cell division and auxin is in charge of plant growth.
Function of auxin: (i)elongation of cell (ii) promote flowering(iii) help in root initiation. etc
2)Similar to this, gibberellin is in charge of stem lengthening, blooming, and fruit ripening.

8. Explain the need of control and coordination in any living organism with examples.
Ans-
The working together of the various organs of an organism in a systematic manner so as to produce a proper response to the stimulus is called coordination.
2)When a stimulus acts upon body of an organism then it has to react in a manner which is in the best interest of its body.
3) The reaction which we give to the stimulus involves many organs of body. It is therefore necessary that all concerned organs should work with one another in a systematic manner

so as to produce the required reaction. For this there should an efficient mechanism for controlling various organs.
ex.-

9. 'Plants are sensitive to light' cite an experiment to justify this statement.
Ans:-
Yes, plants are sensitive to light because if the apical end of the stem of plant receives light from any direction then due to information received by meristematic cells of its opposite direction, cells divide fast, due to which plants bend towards the direction of the incident light.
By this, it is assumed that information's are exchanged in the form of special chemical substance in plants by which its various biological activities are performed. Thus, it proves that plants are sensitive towards light

10. Give examples to show how plants respond to stimuli.
Ans:-
Plants possess the ability to react towards information received through stimulations like water, light, heat, touch, chemical substances etc. This information is transmitted in the form of specific chemicals present in plants, known as plant hormones. In plants, opening and closing of stomata, falling of leaves, increase of rate of division in cells, increase in their length, growth of buds, blossoming of flowers, ripening of flowers are performed by these chemicals.

Example: Auxin found at the apical part of stems of plants is helpful in the growth of cells. Another hormone cytokinin induces cell division. It is found in large amount in fruits and seeds. By the above examples, it proves that plants possess the ability towards stimulation.

Chapter -9

Internal questions

Q-1) Why do metals lose their lustre when left in the open?

Ans-

Metal has soft glow called lustre. It fades away when it is left open in the air because metals make a layer of oxide on the surface by reacting with oxygen in the atmosphere.

Ex.- Magnesium reacts with oxygen to form magnesium oxide

$2Mg + O_2$ —-------> $2MgO$

Q-2) Why are gold and silver used in making ornaments and jewellery?

Ans-gold and silver are metals which reacts least with anything that is why these metals don't lose their shine so these metals are used to make jewellery

Q-3) Write the balanced chemical equations of the reactions of lead, magnesium, aluminium metals with oxygen?

Ans-

Lead reacts with oxygen to form lead oxide.

$2Pb + O_2$ --------> $2PbO$

Magnesium reacts with oxygen to form magnesium oxide

$2Mg + O_2$ -------> $2MgO$

Aluminium react with the oxygen present in air to give aluminium oxides

$4Al + 3O_2$ ------------> $2Al_2O_3$

Q-4) Write the balanced chemical equations for the given reactions:

(a) Reaction of calcium with water

(b) Reaction of iron with steam

Ans-

(a)Reaction of calcium with water: -

Calcium reacts with warm water and produces calcium hydroxide and releases hydrogen gas.

$$Ca + 2H_2O \rightarrow Ca(OH)_2 + H_2 \uparrow$$

(b) Reaction of iron with steam: -

Reaction of iron with steam produces Ferric oxide and releases hydrogen gas.

$$2Fe(s) + 3H_2O(g) \rightarrow \underset{\text{(Ferric oxide)}}{Fe_2O_3(s)} + 3H_2$$

Q-5) What gas is formed when aluminium metal reacts with dilute hydrochloric acid? Write the equation for the reaction

Ans-

Aluminium reacts with dilute hydrochloric acid to form aluminium chloride and hydrogen gas.

$2Al(s) + 6HCl(aq) \rightarrow 2AlCl_3(aq) + 3H_2(g)$.

Q-6) What is aqua regia?

Ans-

Aqua regia is a mixture of nitric acid and hydrochloric acid, optimally in a molar ratio of 1:3. Gold and platinum react only with aqua-regia

$$HNO_3 + 3\ HCl \rightarrow Cl_3H_4NO_3$$

Q-7) Write the names and chemical formulae of oxide ores of iron.

Ans:-

Name of ore	Formula of ore
Oxide Hematite	Fe_2O_3
Magnetite	Fe_3O_4

Q-8) How are sulphide ores concentrated?

Ans-

The heating of concentrated sulphide ore a little below its melting point in the presence of air or oxygen is known as roasting. During roasting, the impurities are vaporized which eases the reduction of the metal compound. Roasting is usually carried out for sulphide ores.

$$2ZnS + 3O_2 \longrightarrow 2ZnO + 2SO_2$$

Q-9) Na, K and Ca metals are obtained from their compounds using electrolysis, why

Ans:-

Na, K and Ca metals are obtained from their compounds using electrolysis because these are highly reactive metals so they make compound with most of element in nature, so they could not be obtained easily by thermal and chemical reduction methods. so When electric current is passed through these compounds, the cation dissociates from the anion and is reduced to the corresponding metal at the cathode. This process is known as electrolysis.

Q-10) Which reactions are helpful in maintaining high temperatures within the blast furnace?

Ans-

Coke reacts with oxygen to form carbon dioxide gas. Since excess of coke is added, therefore the extra coke reacts with carbon dioxide gas to form carbon monoxide. Coke also reacts with insufficient oxygen to form carbon monoxide. This process ensures that high temperature (400°C900°C) is maintained within the furnace.

$$C + O2 \rightarrow CO_2$$

$$CO2 + C \rightarrow 2CO$$

$2C + O_2 \rightarrow 2CO$

Oxide ores react with carbon monoxide gas to give iron and carbon dioxide. This reaction is exothermic.

$Fe_2O_3 + 3CO \rightarrow 2Fe + 3CO_2$

Since this reaction maintains high temperature in the furnace therefore the carbon dioxide gas in not allowed to escape and again sent in to react with coke.

Q-11) Which compound is used as flux in the blast furnace during extraction or iron metal?

Ans-

. The calcium oxide formed during the reaction is used to remove impurities from the ore and is known as flux. The flux reacts with silica to form calcium silicate, also known as slag.

$$CaCO_3 \rightarrow CaO + CO_2$$

$$\underset{\text{Flux}}{CaO} + \underset{\text{impurity}}{SiO_2} \rightarrow \underset{\text{slag}}{CaSiO_3}$$

Since the furnace temperature is kept between 1200°C and 1600°C, iron and calcium silicate remain in molten state. Their densities being different, they collect in two layers at the bottom of the furnace and are removed through outlets at two different layers.

Q-12)How will the rate of corrosion be affected in water that has a high concentration of salts?

Ans-

The process of corrosion is actually an electrochemical process. When metals like iron are placed in air and humid conditions then negatively and positively charged regions develop on its surface because of which it starts behaving like an electrochemical cell.

When water has high concentration of salt it creates positive and negative regions very fast so rate of corrosion increases.

Q-13) Why do we make alloys?

Ans-. A homogeneous mixture in which at least one of the primary components is a metal is called an alloy. Alloying is done to increase hardness, improve quality or decrease melting point. Alloys can be easily cast or moulded into different shapes and find uses in many areas.

Q-14) What is galvanization?

Ans-

Corrosion of metal can also be prevented by using a more reactive metal. This process is known as sacrificial protection or galvanization.

For example- galvanized iron where the iron object is coated with a thin layer of zinc metal. Zinc being more reactive than iron, reacts more readily with oxygen and a thick layer of ZnO is formed which prevents the rusting of iron.

Exercise question

3) Explain the following: -
(i) Ore: Ore is a naturally occurring material from which a metal or valuable mineral can be extracted profitably. Ores typically contain minerals, which are compounds of metals in combination with other elements. The process of extracting the metal from the ore is called metallurgy.
(ii) Mineral: A mineral is a naturally occurring inorganic solid with a definite chemical composition and a specific internal structure. Minerals are often the constituents of ores. They can be made up of various elements and compounds.
(iii) Slag: Slag is the waste material produced in the extraction of a metal from its ore. It consists of impurities and non-metallic compounds that are separated from the metal during the extraction process. Slag is usually formed as a molten material and solidifies as it cools.
(iv) Flux: A flux is a substance that is used to lower the melting point of the metal oxides present in the ore during the process of metallurgy. It helps in the removal of impurities from the ore and facilitates the formation of a slag. Common fluxes include limestone (calcium carbonate) and silica.
4) Balanced chemical equations for the given reactions:

(i) **Reaction of aluminium metal with steam:
$2Al + 3H_2O \rightarrow Al_2O_3 + 3H_2$

(ii) **Reaction of zinc oxide with sodium hydroxide:
$ZnO + 2NaOH \rightarrow Na_2ZnO_2 + H_2O$

(iii) Reaction when calcium carbonate is heated:
$CaCO_3(s) \rightarrow CaO(s) + CO_2(g)$

(iv) **Reaction of oxygen with sodium:
$4Na + O_2 \rightarrow 2Na_2O$

5) Explanation of the process of reduction of metal from a metal oxide:
The reduction of a metal from its oxide involves the removal of oxygen from the metal oxide. This is typically done by using a reducing agent. Common reducing agents include carbon (in the form of coke or charcoal), hydrogen, or other metals. The reduction process can be summarized as:

Metal Oxide (MOx) + Reducing Agent (R) → Metal (M) + By-products

For example, in the extraction of iron from iron ore (Fe_2O_3), carbon (in the form of coke) is used as the reducing agent in a blast furnace:

$Fe2O3 + 3C \rightarrow 2Fe + 3CO$

6) Methods to prevent corrosion:
Barrier Protection: Applying a physical barrier, such as paint, oil, or grease, on the metal surface to block contact with moisture and oxygen.

Galvanization: Coating the metal with a layer of zinc, which acts as a sacrificial anode and corrodes instead of the underlying metal.
Corrosion Inhibitors: Adding chemicals that react with the metal surface to form a protective layer that prevents corrosion. Examples include chromates and phosphates.

Alloying: Mixing metals to create alloys that are more corrosion-resistant than pure metals. For instance, stainless steel contains chromium, which forms a protective oxide layer. These methods help in reducing or preventing the corrosion of metals, which can save resources and extend the lifespan of structures and equipment.

7) In the purification of a metal (M), what all will act as anode, cathode, and electrolyte. Explain with an example:

In the purification of a metal through the process of electrolysis, anode, cathode, and electrolyte play specific roles:

Anode: The anode is the positive electrode where oxidation (loss of electrons) occurs. It is typically made of an inert substance (one that does not react chemically with the metal ions) or the impure metal to be purified.

Cathode: The cathode is the negative electrode where reduction (gain of electrons) takes place. It is usually made of a highly pure metal that the process aims to produce.

Electrolyte: The electrolyte is the solution that contains the metal salt from which the metal is to be extracted. It is necessary for the flow of ions during the process. The electrolyte provides metal ions to the cathode and receives metal ions from the anode.

Example: Purification of Copper through Electrolysis

In the purification of copper, impure copper acts as the anode, pure copper acts as the cathode, and a solution of copper sulphate serves as the electrolyte. When an electric current is passed through the system, copper ions from the anode move into the electrolyte, and pure copper ions from the electrolyte are deposited on the cathode, resulting in the purification of copper.

8) Explain the following techniques used in the concentration of ore:

(i)Gravity Separation Method:

- This technique relies on the differences in the densities of the ore and gangue (unwanted materials). It is effective for separating minerals with a significant difference in density.
- Ore is crushed and fed onto a sloping table. Heavier ore particles settle to the bottom, while lighter gangue particles are washed away.
- Example: Separation of gold particles from sand or gravel in a gold pan.

(ii) Froth Flotation Method:

- This technique is used when ore particles are hydrophobic (repel water) while gangue particles are hydrophilic (attracted to water).
- A mixture of water, ore, and chemicals (collectors and frothers) is agitated. Air is bubbled through the mixture, and the hydrophobic ore particles attach to the air bubbles and form a froth, which is skimmed off.
- A layer of pine oil is formed on the surface of the sulphide ore particles which causes the air bubbles to stick to them. The ore particles come to the surface with the froth while impurities like soil, pebbles, stones etc. settle down
- Example: Separation of sulphide ores like copper, lead, and zinc from their gangue.

(iii) Magnetic Separation Method:

This method can be used if magnetic substances are present in the ore. In this method, the finely ground ore is passed over a conveyor belt which is stretched over magnetic rollers. The magnetic particles remain stuck to the belt till they are moved away from the magnetic effect of the roller whereas the non-magnetic particles fall from the belt as soon as it starts moving. In this way, two heaps are obtained; one heap is of magnetic material and the other is of non-magnetic material

These techniques are used to separate valuable minerals from the waste material (gangue) in ores, making it easier to extract the desired metal during the subsequent

9) Discuss the extraction of iron from hematite as per the following steps: (i) Concentration of ore (ii) Reduction of oxide to metal (along with chemical equation) (iii) Diagram of blast furnace

Ans:-

(i)concentration of ore: -

Hematite (Fe_2O_3) is a type of iron ore. The concentration of hematite involves the removal of impurities and gangue materials to obtain concentrated iron ore. This is typically done through the following steps:

Crushing and grinding the ore into fine powder.

Magnetic separation: Magnetic separators are used to separate magnetic ore from non-magnetic impurities.

Gravity separation: The heavy iron ore particles settle at the bottom, and the lighter gangue materials are washed away. Top of Form

(ii) Reduction of oxide in metal: For reduction smelting process is used and it is done in blast furnace

Smelting of roasted ore: Roasted ore is smelted with coke (C) and lime stone ($CaCO2$) in blast furnace. As the charge goes down it has to pass through different temperatures 200 to 1600 degree Celsius. The chemical reactions take place in blast furnace are:

A. Combustion of Coke: Coke, which is primarily carbon, is used as a fuel in the blast furnace. It reacts with oxygen from the hot air blown into the furnace to produce carbon dioxide (CO2). This reaction provides the heat necessary for the other reactions in the furnace.

- Reaction: $2C(s) + O_2(g) \rightarrow 2CO\ (g)$

B) Reduction of Iron Ore:The main purpose of the blast furnace is to reduce iron ore (usually hematite, Fe2O3) to molten iron. This reduction process occurs at high temperatures in the lower part of the furnace, where carbon monoxide (CO) acts as the reducing agent. The iron ore is reduced to molten iron, and impurities combine with the flux (limestone) to form slag.

- Reaction: $Fe_2O_3(s) + 3CO(g) \rightarrow 2Fe(l) + 3CO_2(g)$

C) Formation of Slag: Impurities in the iron ore, such as silica (SiO_2), combine with the calcium oxide (CaO) from the limestone ($CaCO_3$) to form calcium silicate ($CaSiO_3$), which constitutes the slag. The slag is lighter than molten iron and is removed from the furnace separately.

- Reaction: $CaCO_3(s) \rightarrow CaO(s) + CO_2(g)$
- Reaction: $CaO(s) + SiO_2(s) \rightarrow CaSiO_3(l)$

These are the fundamental reactions in a blast furnace for the extraction of iron. The heat generated by the combustion of coke drives the reduction of iron ore, leading to the production of molten iron and slag. The molten iron sinks to the bottom of the furnace and is periodically tapped off, while the lighter slag floats on top and is also removed.

diagam:-

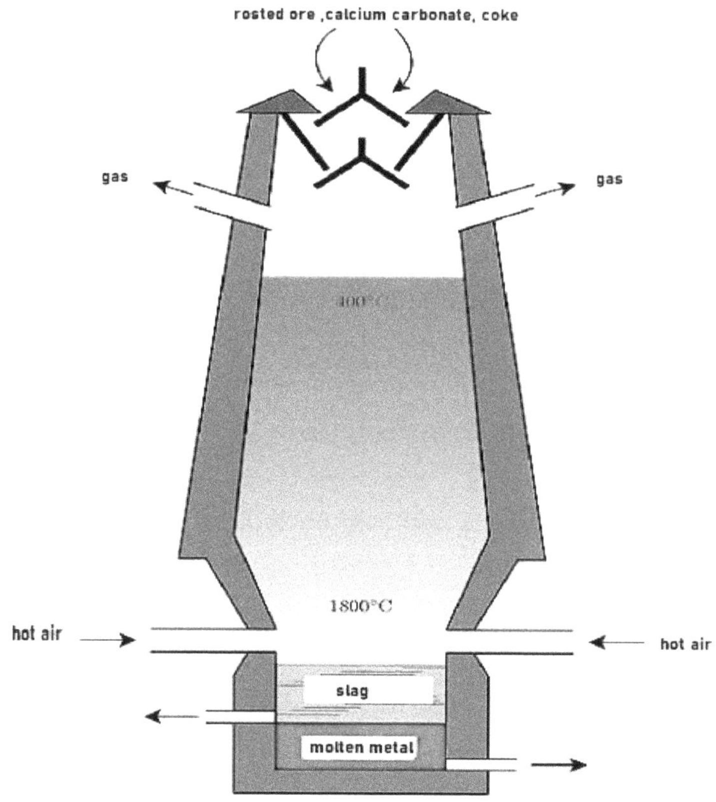

10) Explain the electrochemical principle behind corrosion

Ans:-

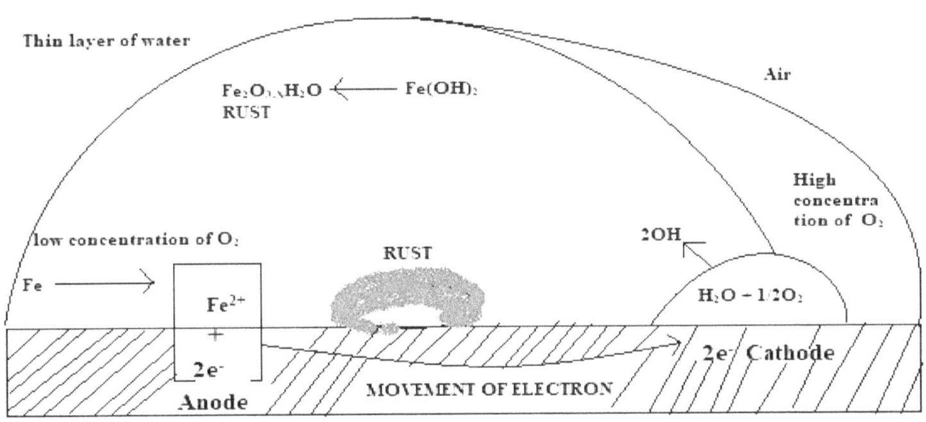

Certainly, let's explain the electrochemical principle behind corrosion with chemical equations, focusing on the rusting of iron as an example:

1. **Anode Reaction:Iron (Fe) undergoes oxidation at the anode, releasing electrons:

$Fe(s) \rightarrow Fe^{2+}(aq) + 2e^-$

In this reaction, solid iron (Fe) loses electrons (e^-) to become iron ions (Fe^{2+}) in an aqueous solution.

2.Electron Flow: The electrons released in the anode reaction flow through the metal, creating an electric current.

3. Cathode Reaction: In the presence of oxygen (O_2) and water (H_2O), reduction of oxygen occurs at the cathode:

$O_2(g) + 4e^- + 2H_2O(l) \rightarrow 4OH^-(aq)$

Oxygen gas (O_2) gains electrons (e^-) and reacts with water (H_2O) to form hydroxide ions (OH^-).

4. Formation of Iron Hydroxide: The iron ions (Fe^{2+}) formed at the anode migrate through the aqueous solution and react with hydroxide ions (OH^-) to form iron hydroxide:

$Fe^{2+}(aq) + 2OH^-(aq) \rightarrow Fe(OH)_2(s)$

Iron ions combine with hydroxide ions to form iron hydroxide, which is a white or greenish precipitate.

5. This iron hydroxide reacts with the oxygen in the atmosphere in the presence of moisture to give hydrated iron oxide.

$$2Fe(OH)_2 + \frac{1}{2} O_2 (g) + H_2O(l) \rightarrow Fe_2 O_3.xH_2O(s)$$

This hydrated iron oxide is known as rust.

It's important to note that corrosion is an ongoing process, and rusting can continue as long as oxygen and moisture are present.

11) . Give reasons for:

(i) Gold, silver, and platinum are used in making jewellery:

Gold, silver, and platinum are used in jewellery because they are unreactive and do not corrode. Their stability is due to their noble or precious metal nature. Here's an example using gold:

Gold does not react with oxygen or moisture in the air, so it remains shiny and untarnished.

Chemical equation: $Au(s) + O_2(g) + H_2O(l) \rightarrow$ No significant reaction

(ii) Sodium, potassium, and lithium metals are stored under kerosene:

These alkali metals are highly reactive with air and moisture, so they are stored under kerosene to prevent contact with these substances. Here's an example using sodium:

Sodium rapidly reacts with oxygen and moisture to form sodium oxide and sodium hydroxide.

Chemical equation: $4Na(s) + O_2(g) + 2H_2O(l) \rightarrow 4NaOH(aq)$

(iii) Although aluminium is an active metal, it is still used to prepare cooking utensils:

Aluminium is an active metal, but it readily forms a protective oxide layer when exposed to air. This oxide layer prevents further corrosion. Here's an example:

Aluminium reacts with oxygen to form a thin, transparent layer of aluminium oxide.

Chemical equation: $4Al(s) + 3O_2(g) \rightarrow 2Al_2O_3(s)$

(iv) Carbonate and sulphide ores are converted into their oxides for the extraction of metal:

The conversion of ores to oxides is often done as a preliminary step in metal extraction. Here's an example using zinc blende (sphalerite):

Zinc sulphide (ZnS) ore is converted to zinc oxide (ZnO) by heating in the presence of air:

Chemical equation: $2ZnS(s) + 3O_2(g) \rightarrow 2ZnO(s) + 2SO_2(g)$

The zinc oxide is then reduced to obtain the pure metal zinc using a suitable reducing agent.

.

Chapter - 10

Q-1) State the laws of reflection ...?

Ans- The process through which light rays fall on the surface and get bounced back is known as a reflection of light. Which is governed by following laws -

1. Angle of incidence is always equal to the angle of reflection.

   $<i = <r$.

2. Incident ray, normal and the reflected ray lie in the same plane.

(Q-2) What are the laws of refraction?

Ans- Refraction is the bending of a wave when it passes from one medium to another. The bending is caused due to the differences in density between the two substances.

Laws of refraction -

The incident ray refracted ray, and the normal to the interface of two media at the point of incidence all lie on the same plane.

The ratio of the sine of the angle of incidence to the sine of the angle of refraction is a constant. This is also known as Snell's law of refraction.

$$\frac{\sin i}{\sin r} = \text{constant}$$

(Q-3) The refractive indices of medium A and B are n_A and n_B respectively. Total internal reflection is possible on going form which medium to which medium given that $n_A > n_B$.

Ans-

Given $n_A > n_B$. which means – $n_A = \frac{c}{vA} \Rightarrow vA = \frac{c}{nA}$

And $n_B = \frac{c}{VB} \Rightarrow V_B = \frac{c}{nB}$

So ($v_A < v_B$) lights speed will be lesser in medium B. than A.

Which means that medium A is optically denser than medium B. the necessary condition for for total internal reflection is that light should travel from denser medium to rarer medium. So in this case light should travel from medium A to medium B to get total internal reflection.

Q-4) What is total internal refraction and what are the necessary conditions for it to take place?

Ans-

when light passes from denser medium to rarer medium and the incident angle is more than the critical angle then light gets internally reflected in the denser medium. This is known as Total Internal Reflection.

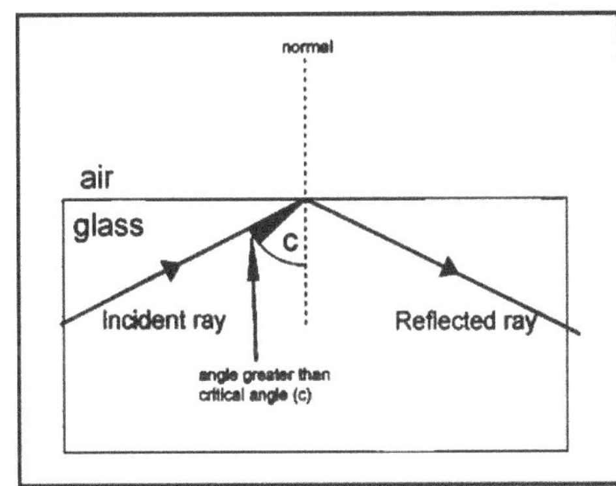

Necessary conditions for total internal reflection: -

1. Light should pass from denser medium to rarer medium.
2. Incident angle should be more than critical angle.

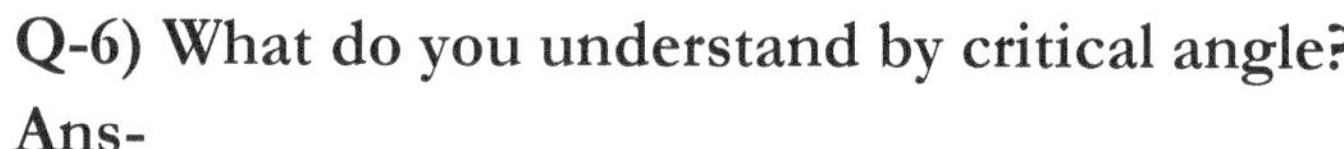

Q-6) What do you understand by critical angle?

Ans-

Def.- The critical angle is the angle of incidence, for which the angle of refraction is 90°.

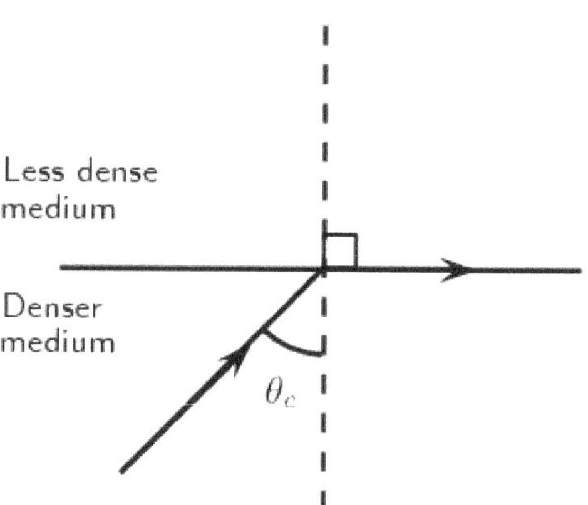

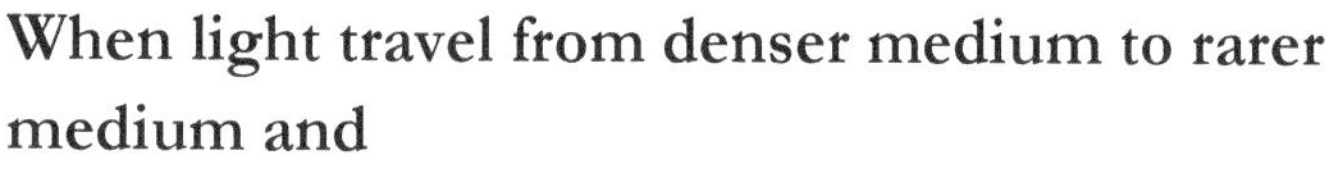

When light travel from denser medium to rarer medium and

For a particular value of incident angle, emergent refracted ray will graze through the surface separating both mediums.

This angle is known as critical angle of that material.

Q-7) Light travels from air to glass slab having refractive index of 1.50. What will be the speed of light in glass? Speed of light in vacuum is 3×10^8 m/s.

Ans-

Given - refractive index $\mu_g = 1.5$

Speed of light in vacuum is $c = 3\times10^8$ m/s

$$\mu_g = \frac{c}{v_g}$$ (where v_g = velocity of light in glass)

$$\text{So} \quad v_g = \frac{c}{\mu_g}$$

$$v_g = \frac{3\times10^8}{1.5} = 2 \times 10^8 \text{ m/s}$$ ans.

Q- (8) Refractive index of diamond is 2.42. Explain this statement.

Ans-

Refractive index - give def. ....

Light speed in diamond will be 1.24×10^8 m/s.

So the refractive index of diamond is 2.42, that is highest. The optical density is directly dependent on the refractive index. Thus, the diamond is the material that has maximum optical density.

Which means compared to any other medium diamond will be denser medium and when light incidents at particular angle Which Is more than critical angle then when light ray tries to go out Of the diamond, total internal reflection occurs and with proper cuts in diamond light rays are being reflected continuously, which gives the diamond the special glare that it has.

Q- (11). A light ray travelling in the air enters the Ice. Will the light ray move away from the normal or towards the normal? Why?

Ans-

When light enters from air to ice it will move towards the normal because refractive index of ice (1.31) is greater than air (1) it means that ice is more optically dense than air. according to the refraction law, we know that wen light travels from rarer medium to denser medium after refraction it moves towards the normal.

Q-(12) If we increase the distance between the mirror the object then what would be the effect on the distance between the image and the object?

Ans-

We know that according to formation of image by a plane mirror, that the distance between object and image is twice of the distance between object and mirror.

Acc. to diagram here we can see distance between object and Plane Mirror is "d" then image is created at distance "d" at the other side of the mirror. So total distance between object And image is "2d".

So if we increase the distance from "d" To "d+x" then image will be created at distance "d+x" On the other side of the mirror. So then distance between object and image will be "2d+2x". therefore, effect is twice Of the increase in distance between object and mirror.

Q-13. What is the difference between virtual image and real image?

Ans-

Real image	Virtual image

Image is formed when rays of light meet at a point after reflection/refraction is called real image.	Image is formed when rays of light appears to meet (diverging rays when extended) at a point is called virtual image.
Real image are always inverted	Virtual images are always erect
Real images can be obtained on screen	Virtual image can't be obtained on screen
Is is formed by only concave mirror	a virtual image can be formed by concave, convex and plane mirror also.

Q-14. What is the difference between absolute refractive index of a medium and the relative refractive index of two mediums? What is the relation between them?

Ans-

Absolute refractive index-

If the speed of light is 'v' in a medium and 'c' in vacuum, then, the ratio of the speed of light in vacuum to speed of light in the medium is called 'absolute refractive index' of that medium. We denote this by 'n'.

$$\text{Absolute refractive index} = \frac{\text{speed of light in vacuum}}{\text{speed of light in medium}}$$

Relative refractive index-

The ratio of speed of light in the first medium and speed of light in the second medium is called relative refractive index. We denote this by 1μ2 or n21.

$$n21 = \frac{\text{speed of light in first medium}}{\text{speed f light in the second medium}}$$

Relation between absolute and relative refractive index: -

$$n_{21} = \frac{\text{speed of light in first medium}}{\text{speed f light in the second medium}}$$

$$n_{21} = \frac{v1}{v2}$$

$$= \frac{v1/c}{v2/c}$$

$$= \frac{v1}{c} \times \frac{c}{v2}$$

$$= \frac{1}{c/v1} \times n_2$$

$$= \frac{1}{n1} \times n_2$$

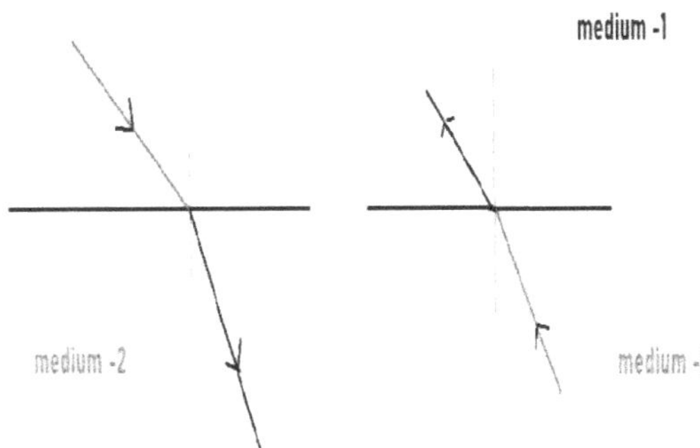

$$n_{21} = n_2 / n_1$$

Q-15. What is the principal of reversibility?

Ans-

The principle of reversibility states that light follows the same path if the direction of light is reversed. It can be understood by snell's law of refraction.

If we have 2 medium - water and glass and light passes from both medium then at the the interface refraction occurs.

When it travels from water to glass -

$$_w\mu_g \text{ or } n_{gw} = \frac{\sin i}{\sin r} \quad \ldots\ldots\ldots\ldots\ldots\ldots(1)$$

And when the direction of light is reversed then

medium -1

medium -2

$$_g\mu_w \text{ or } n_{wg} = \frac{\sin r}{\sin i} \quad \ldots\ldots\ldots\ldots\ldots\ldots(2)$$

When eq. -(1) is multiplied with(2)

$$_w\mu_g \times {_g\mu_w} = \frac{\sin i}{\sin r} \times \frac{\sin r}{\sin i} = 1$$

$$_w\mu_g = 1/ {_g\mu_w}$$

be reciprocal.

Q-16. State the reasons for following: - And relative reflective index of water and glass with respect to each other is fixed so they are reciprocal to each other which also means that the reversed path will also

(i) The position of fish in a pond is not same as it is observed from outside.

(ii) A Bubble of air shines in water.

(iii) Mirage is an illusion.

Ans-

(i) The position of fish in a pond is not same as it is observed from outside.

It is because of the bending of light because of the

fractive index of water is greater than air. Light rays coming form the fish will bend and move away from the normal according to snell's law. As we can see that light rays are diverging

But if we trace them back they appears to meet at a Different point which is above the original depth. Which can be calculated

By - Refractive Index $= \frac{\text{actual depth}}{\text{virtual depth}}$

(ii) A Bubble of air shines in water.

Ans-

It happens because of the total internal reflection. When light ray's incident on the surface of bubble inside water at an angle more than

critical angle (48.8) then total internal Refraction occurs and light reflects back and makes the bubble sparkly.

(iii) Mirage is an illusion.

Ans-

Mirage- During hot days in the deserts, people see an inverted reflection of a distant pine tree which make them believe that there is pool of water around the tree. However, when they reach there they find that there is no water. This illusion is known as mirage. During the day the air near the sand become hotter so it behaves as a rarer medium and upper layer of air remains colder and it behaves as a denser medium.

So when light ray from tree it passes from denser medium to rarer medium and bend away from the normal as shown in the diag. At one stage the incident angle becomes more than the critical angle and light ray gets totally internally reflected. So when this rays are traced back it meets at a point below the tree and an inverted image of tree is created Which creates an illusion of water under the tree.

Q-18. What do you mean by refraction of light? How is it different from reflection of light?

Ans-

refraction: -The change in the direction of a wave when it passes from one medium to another is known as refraction. It happens because of different optical Density of different media. Which causes change in The speed of light.

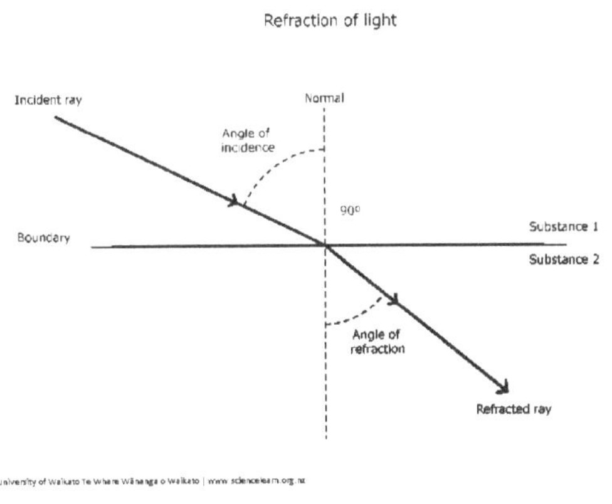

Ex.- The light rays bend as they enter water drops in the atmosphere forming a rainbow.

Reflection-

Reflection is the bouncing back of light when it strikes a smooth surface.Ex.- seeing our self in the mirror.

Chapter -11

Internal question (page 182)

1.What are metalloids? Give any two examples.

Ans:- Metalloids are elements that have properties intermediate between metals and non-metals. They can exhibit characteristics of both categories, making them unique. Two exa mples of metalloids are silicon and germanium.

2.Give reasons why gaseous elements were discovered quite late as compared to solid elements.

Ans:-

Gaseous elements were discovered quite late compared to solid elements because gases are less dense and more difficult to isolate and identify. Early scientists lacked the advanced equipment and techniques needed to capture and study gases, which made their discovery more challenging

3.The elements of group 18 do not normally take part in chemical reactions, why?

Ans:-

The elements of group 18 (also known as noble gases) do not normally take part in cemical reactions because their outermost electron shell is full. This makes them very stable and unreactive, as they do not need to gain, lose, or share electrons to achieve a stable configuration.

Inter question (page 184)

1.Look up the names of different acids used in the laboratory and find out the non-metals that make them up.

1. Ans:- Laboratory acids and their non-metal components:
    - Hydrochloric acid (HCl): Made up of hydrogen and chlorine.
    - Sulphuric acid (H_2SO_4): Made up of hydrogen, sulphur, and oxygen.
    - Nitric acid (HNO_3): Made up of hydrogen, nitrogen, and oxygen.
    - Acetic acid (CH_3COOH): Made up of hydrogen, carbon, and oxygen.
2. Non-metals are electronegative, why?

   Ans:- Non-metals are electronegative because they have a high tendency to attract electrons towards themselves. This is due to their high nuclear charge and smaller atomic radii, which allows them to pull electrons more effectively.

3. You are given an element; how will you identify whether it is a metal or non-metal? **Give three means.**

Ans:- To identify whether an element is a metal or non-metal, you can use the following means:

- Physical properties: Metals are typically shiny, malleable, ductile, and good conductors of heat and ele ctricity. Non-metals, on the other hand, are usually dull, brittle, and poor conductors.
- Chemical properties: Metals tend to lose electrons and form positive ions (cations) in chemical reactio ns, while non-metals tend to gain electrons and form negative ions (anions).
- Position in the periodic table: Metals are generally found on the left side and in the center of the perio dic table, while non-metals are found on the right side

Internal question (page 190)

1.Write the balanced chemical equations for reactions of calcium, lithium and aluminium with hydrogen.

1. Ans:-
   Balanced chemical equations for reactions of calcium, lithium, and aluminum with hydrogen:
   - Calcium: $Ca+H_2 \rightarrow CaH_2$
   - Lithium: $2Li+H_2 \rightarrow 2LiH$
   - Aluminium: $2Al + 3H_2 \rightarrow 2AlH_3$
2. Which gas is used in packaged foods and why?
   Ans:- Nitrogen gas is commonly used in packaged foods because it is inert and helps to displace oxygen, which can cause spoilage and oxidation. By removing oxygen, nitrogen helps to preserve the freshness and extend the shelf life of the food.
3. In laboratories, oxygen is collected in an upturned, water-filled test tube or gas jar, why?
Ans:- In laboratories, oxygen is collected in an upturned, water-filled test tube or gas jar because oxygen is slightly soluble in water and less dense than water
.
This method allows the oxygen gas to displace the water and be collected without conta mination from other gases.

Exercise

1. Choose the correct option:
 (i) The solution in water of which of the following will be acidic:
   - (b) CO2
 (ii) Which of the following elements does not exhibit allotropy:
   - (a) Sodium

(iii) Which among the following is a metalloid:
   - (d) Arsenic

(iv) Noble gases do not react with other elements because:

- (c) Their outermost shell is full

(v) The gas obtained on heating potassium permanganate is:

- (b) Oxygen

2) Fill in the blanks:

(i) The most electronegative element is fluorine.

(ii) Carbon is less reactive as compared to oxygen.

(iii) Non-metals are found at the right side of the periodic table.

(iv) Hydrogen gas is obtained when granulated zinc is reacted with dilute acid or alkali.

3. Compare the physical properties of metals and non-metals.

Ans:-

metals	non-metals
Metals: ○ Generally shiny (lustrous). ○ Good conductors of heat and electricity. ○ Malleable (can be hammered into thin sh eets). ○ Ductile (can be drawn into wires). ○ High melting and boiling points	○ Generally dull (non-lustrous). ○ Poor conductors of heat and electri city. ○ Brittle (break easily when hammer ed). ○ Non-ductile. ○ Low melting and boiling points

4. Write the balanced chemical equations for formation of chlorides and oxides of the following elements - hydrogen, phosphorous, sodium and magnesium.

Ans:- Hydrogen:

- Chloride: $H_2+Cl_2 \rightarrow 2HCl$
- Oxide: $2H_2+O_2 \rightarrow 2H_2O$

- Phosphorus:
  - Chloride: $2P+3Cl_2 \rightarrow 2PCl_3$
  - Oxide: $4P+5O_2 \rightarrow 2P_2O_5$
- Sodium:
  - Chloride: $2Na+Cl_2 \rightarrow 2NaCl$
  - Oxide: $4Na+O_2 \rightarrow 2Na_2O$
- Magnesium:
  - Chloride: $Mg+Cl_2 \rightarrow MgCl_2$
  - Oxide: $2Mg+O_2 \rightarrow 2MgO$

5. Write the equation and corresponding conditions for reaction between nitrogen and hydrogen.

Ans:- Equation and conditions for reaction between nitrogen and hydrogen:

- Equation: $N_2+3H_2 \rightarrow 2NH_3$
- Conditions: This reaction, known as the Haber process, requires high pressure (around 200 atmospheres), high temperature (around 450°C), and the presence of an iron catalyst.

6. "Hydrogen can be placed either in group 1 or in group 17". Do you agree with this statement or disagree? Give reasons.

Ans:- hydrogen can be placed either in group 1 or in group 17. Here's why:

- Group 1 (Alkali metals): Hydrogen has one electron in its outermost shell, simi lar to alkali metals, which also have one electron in their outermost shell. This allows hydrogen to form positive ions (H^+) like alkali metals.
- Group 17 (Halogens): Hydrogen can also gain one electron to achieve a stable electron configuration, similar to halogens, which need one electron to comple te their outermost shell. This allows hydrogen to form negative ions (H^-) like h alogens.

7. Why are helium, neon, krypton, argon, xenon and radon known as inert gases?

Ans:-

Helium, neon, krypton, argon, xenon, and radon are known as inert gases (or noble gases) because they are extremely unreactive. This lack of reactivity is due to their full outer electr on shells, which make them very stable. They don't need to gain, lose, or share electrons to achieve a stable configuration, so they rarely form compounds with other elements. This sta bility is what makes them "inert."

8. Explain the following industrial uses of hydrogen-

(a) Heat production on combustion (b) Reaction with vegetable oils in the presence of a catalyst

Ans:- Industrial uses of hydrogen:

(a) Heat production on combustion: Hydrogen is used as a fuel because it produc es a significant amount of heat when it combusts. The reaction is highly exoth ermic, and the only byproduct is water, making it an environmentally friendly option. The balanced chemical equation for the combustion of hydrogen is: $2H_2+O_2 \rightarrow 2H_2O$

(b) Reaction with vegetable oils in the presence of a catalyst: Hydrogen is used in the hydrogenation of vegetable oils to produce margarine and other hydrogenated fats. This process involves adding hydrogen to the carbon-carbon double bonds in unsaturated fats, converting them into saturated fats. The reaction is typically carried out in the presence of a nickel catalyst. The general equation for the hydrogenation of an unsaturated fat (R-CH=CH-R') is:

$$R\text{-}CH{=}CH\text{-}R' + H_2 \rightarrow R\text{-}CH_2\text{-}CH_2\text{-}R'$$

9. What happens when potassium permanganate is heated? Explain giving balanced equation.

Ans:-

When potassium permanganate ($KMnO_4$) is heated, it decomposes to form potassium man ganate (K_2MnO_4), manganese dioxide (MnO_2), and oxygen gas (O_2). The balanced chemic al equation for this decomposition reaction is:

$$2KMnO_4 \rightarrow K_2MnO_4 + MnO_2 + O_2$$

10.Gas 'A' is formed when granulated zinc reacts with dilute hydrochloric acid. It reacts with oxide 'B' and reduces it to copper metal. Write the names of 'A' and 'B' and also give the equations for the described reactions.

Ans:-

Gas 'A' is hydrogen (H2), and oxide 'B' is copper(II) oxide (CuO). The reactions are as foll ows:

- Reaction of zinc with hydrochloric acid:
  $Zn + 2HCl \rightarrow ZnCl_2 + H_2$
- Reaction of hydrogen with copper(II) oxide:
  $H_2 + CuO \rightarrow Cu + H_2O$

11. Sevati took sulphur powder in deflagrating spoon, heated it and collected the gas formed in a test tube. What will happen when moist red and blue litmus papers are taken near the mouth of the test tube and why? Write the chemical equations for the reactions taking place.

Ans:-

When Sevati heats sulfur powder and collects the gas formed (sulfur dioxide, SO2), and brin gs moist red and blue litmus papers near the mouth of the test tube:

- The moist red litmus paper will remain red.
- The moist blue litmus paper will turn red. This happens because sulfur dioxid e dissolves in water to form sulfurous acid (H2SO3), which is acidic. The che mical equations are:

  $S + O_2 \rightarrow SO_2$

  $SO_2 + H_2O \rightarrow H_2SO_3$

12. The processes described below are due to which property of hydrogen

(a) A hydrogen filled balloon floats in air. (b). A 'pop' sound is heard when a lighted matchstick is taken near the mouth of a hydrogen filled gas jar.

3. Ans:-

   - A hydrogen-
     filled balloon floats in air: This is because hydrogen is less dense than air.

- A 'pop' sound is heard when a lighted matchstick is taken near the mouth of a hydrogen-
filled gas jar: This is due to the explosive nature of hydrogen when it reacts wit h oxygen in the air to form water. The reaction is:

$$2H_2+O_2 \rightarrow 2H_2O$$

13. Compound X, which is used for drinking, has pH value 7. Electrolysis of an acidic solution of X gives gases Y and Z. The volume of Y is twice that of Z. Y burns rapidly while Z supports burning. Identify X, Y and Z and write the equations for the described reactions
Ans:- Compound X is water (H_2O), gas Y is hydrogen (H_2), and gas Z is oxygen (O_2). The volume of hydrogen is twice that of oxygen because water is composed of two hydrogen at oms and one oxygen atom. The reactions during electrolysis are:

- At the cathode (reduction):

$$2H^++2e^- \rightarrow H_2$$

- At the anode (oxidation): $2O^{2-} \rightarrow O_2+4e^-$

Chapter -12

Q. 1. What is Magnetic lines of force?

Ans.

Magnetic lines of force around a magnet is graphical representation of magnetic field and it gives direction and magnitude of magnetic field.

Q. 2. State the properties of magnetic lines of force.

Ans.

(i) They always start from north pole and terminate at south pole.

(ii) These are straight or curved lines, tangent drawn at any point of which gives the direction of intensity of magnetic field at that point.

(iii) They repel each other.

(iv) Magnetic lines of force are closer at the poles and are far apart at neutral axis.

(v) Magnetic lines of force are smooth curves drawn in a magnetic field.

(vi) Two magnetic lines of force never intersect.

Q. 3 Draw magnetic field lines of a straight current carrying conductor wire.

Ans-

here right circular magnetic field has been generated.

Q. 4. The current in a wire is flowing from East to West direction. What will be the direction of magnetic field at a point just below and just above the wire?

Ans.

Current through the wire is flowing from East to West direction. Then according to Fleming's Right Hand Rule at a point just below the wire, fingers will point the direction of magnetic field is south and at a point just above it will be north, thumb will show the direction of current.

Q. 7. Activity: Suspend a small rod AB of aluminium using connecting wires with a stand. Place a strong horse shoe type magnet such that the rod lies l? between the poles of magnet and the magnetic field be directed vertically upwards. For this N-pole should be below the rod and S-pole be placed above the

Now pass current through the rod (from During activity how the displacement of rod will change if (a) Current through this be increased?

(b) Another stronger horse shoe type magnet be used? (c) Length of the rod be reduced?

Ans.

(a) If our-rent through rod AB be increased, then it displaces towards left and the direction of force exerted on current carrying conductor changes.

(b)If another stronger but of same strength horse shoe type magnet be used, no change in displacement of AB will be noticed.

(c)If length of the rod be reduced, no change in displacement will be seen.

Q. 8. What is electric motor? (C.G. 2017 Set A, B, C)

Ans.

It is a device which converts electrical energy into mechanical energy. It is used in electric fans, refrigerators, washing machines, computers, mixers etc.

Q. 9. What is the principle of electric motor?

Ans. Electric motor works on the principle that a current carving conductor placed in a magnetic field experiences a magnetic force which can rotate the conductor about an axis.

Q. 10. State Fleming's Left Hand Rule.

Ans.

According to Fleming's Left Hand Rule, the thumb, central finger and fore finger of the left hand be stretched in mutually perpendicular directions and the fore finger be pointed along the direction of magnetic field, central finger pointed in the direction of current then thumb will point along the direction of magnetic force on the conductor.

Q. 11. What is the role of split rings in electric motor?

Ans. In electric motor split ring commutator reverses the flow of electric current. On reversing the direction of current, the forces on arms AB and CD of coil of electric motor also reverses due to which coil continuously rotates on its axis.

Q. 12. What is electric generator?

Ans:- It is a device which converts mechanical energy into electrical energy. It is called A.C. Dynamo or electric generator.

Q. 13. State the principle of electric generator.

Ans. Electric generator works on the principle of electromagnetic induction. When a coil is rotated in a strong magnetic field then number of magnetic lines of force linked with the coil change, as a result of which induced electric current starts flowing through the coil.

Q. 14. What is split ring commutator?

Ans. In electric generator two ends of rectangular coil, are connected with rings RI and R2 which are internally joined with the axis of armature. Two rings RI and R2 are called split ring commutator. So that we get a a.c. current.

Q. 15. What will happen if a rod of soft iron be buried in the earth along geographic North-South direction?
Ans.

If a rod of soft iron be buried in the earth along North-South direction for some days, then it also starts behaving like a magnet i.e. the rod will exhibit magnetic properties. The end of the rod towards geographic North will behave like South pole and vice-versa.

Exercise

1. Choose the correct option (ans. Is in capital)
(i) The magnetic lines of force determine,
(a) shape of the magnetic field (b) DIRECTION OF THE FIELD (c) intensity of the magnetic field (d) intensity and direction of magnetic field
(ii) A straight current carrying conductor has a magnetic field
(a) lines of force parallel to the conductor (b) lines of force perpendicular to the conductor
(c) LINES OF FORCE IN CONCENTRIC CIRCLES AROUND THE CONDUCTOR
(d) lines of force starting radially from the wire end
(iii) A solenoid has a magnetic field inside it, which is
(a) different at each point (b) SAME AT EACH POINT (c) zero (d) None of the above
(iv) electromagnetic induction is a phenomenon to
(a) charge any matter (b) rotate a coil (c) produce magnetic field in a coil (d) TO PRODUCE INDUCED CURRENT WHEN EITHER COIL OR MAGNET MOVES.
(v) We can generate electric current using– (a) GENERATOR (b) Motor (c) Galvanometer (d) Ammeter

2. Fill in the blanks
(i) That device which converts mechanical energy into electrical energy is generator
(ii)electric motor converts electrical energy into mechanical energy.
(iii) Fleming's left hand rule indicates the direction of force on conductor
(iv) Fleming's right hand rule indicates the direction of induced current. acting on the conductor.
(v) Maxwell's left hand rule indicates the direction of magnetic field.
q-4) A magnetic field is created around a conductor when current flows in it. Which scientist first confirmed this phenomenon?
Ans. H.C. Oersted.
Q. 5. Write the right hand rule of Fleming.
Ans. According to this rule, if we spread the thumb, the first finger and the middle finger of the right hand in such a way that they are perpendicular to each other., then The thumb represents the direction of motion of the conductor, first finger shows the direction of

magnetic field lines of force and the middle finger points in the direction of the flow of induced current.

Q. 6. Name three devices which make use of electric motor.

Ans. Electric fans, refrigerators, washing. machines, computers, mixer etc.

Q.7. List the three ways in which a magnetic field can be produced.

Ans. (i) Magnetic field is produced on passing current through a straight conductor.

(ii)Magnetic field produced due to a current carrying circular loop of wire.

(iii)Magnetic field produced due to current flowing through a solenoid.

Q. 8. How does a solenoid act as a magnet? Can you determine its North and South poles by help of a bar magnet?

Ans. Solenoid is a cylindrical coil of a large number of insulated copper wire. The magnetic field produced by a current carrying solenoid is similar to the magnetic field of a bar magnet. Therefore, current carrying solenoid behaves like a bar magnet, north and south poles at opposite ends.

So the side which repels north pole of bar magnet would be north of solenoid.

Q. 9. Write three properties of a magnet.

Ans. (i) Magnet attracts materials like iron, nickel etc.

(ii)A freely suspended magnet always rests in north-south direction.

(iii)If a magnet be cut into small pieces then also each part behaves like an individual magnet.

Q. 10. What are magnetic lines of force? Give three properties.

Ans. Magnetic lines of force around a magnet is graphical representation of magnetic field and it gives direction and magnitude of magnetic field.

(i) They always start from north pole and terminate at south pole.

(ii) These are straight or curved lines, tangent drawn at any point of which gives the direction of intensity of magnetic field at that point.

(iii) They repel each other.

Q. 11. Why do two magnetic lines of force not intersect each other?

Ans. If two lines of force intersect then two tangents can be drawn at point of intersection i.e. resultant force will have two directions, which is impossible. Therefore, two magnetic lines of force do not intersect.

Q. 12. Discuss electric motor under the following heads:

(a) Labelled diagram, (b) Principle, (c) Working.

Ans-

Labelled diagram: -

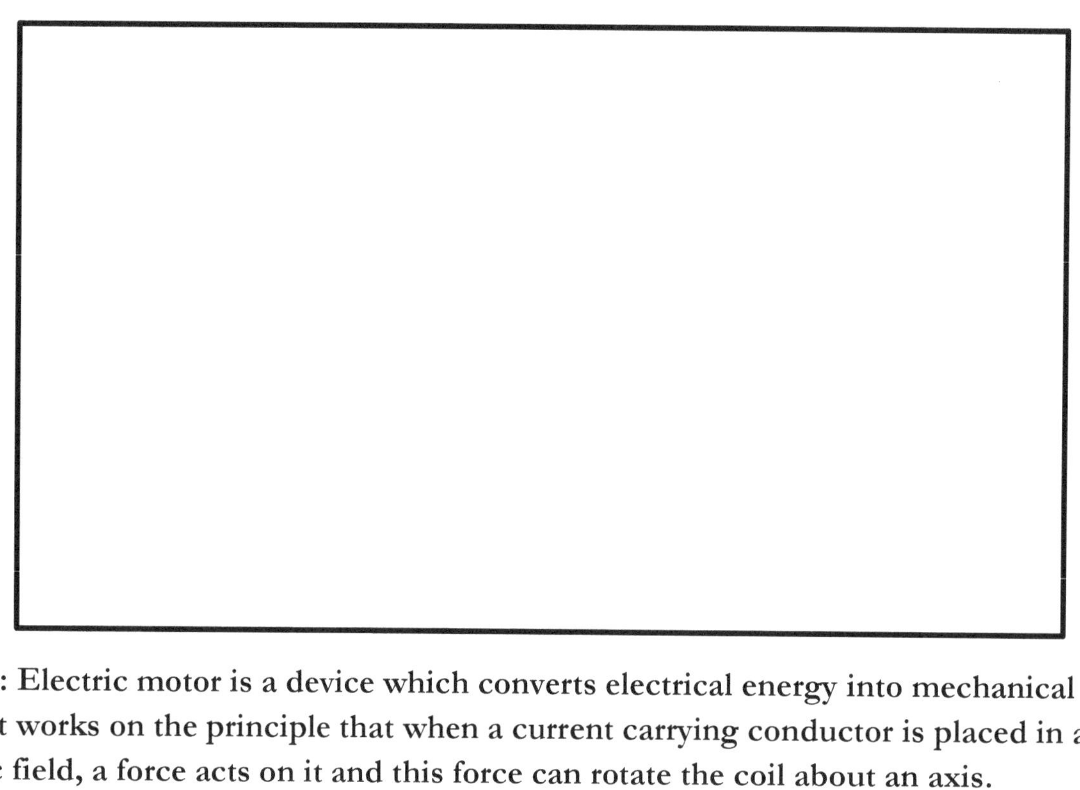

Principle: Electric motor is a device which converts electrical energy into mechanical energy. It works on the principle that when a current carrying conductor is placed in a magnetic field, a force acts on it and this force can rotate the coil about an axis.

Working: It consists of a rectangular coil (PQRS) of insulated copper wire. This coil is mounted on a rectangular frame, known as armature. Armature is free to rotate about its own axis in a place between two concave shape pole pieces of a permanent magnet. Ends of armature are connected with two split rings S1 and S2.

Source of current and key are connected with split rings through the carbon brushes. Let at one instant of time armature PQRS be in horizontal position. As shown in figure, when current is passed through the coil then according to Fleming's Left Hand Rule a downward force acts on arms PQ and upward force acts on RS. Thus, it forms a couple and rotates the coil in clockwise direction. After half revolution S1 , and S2 interchange their positions, due to which PQ moves up and RS goes down. In this way, coil rotates continuously.

Q-13. Describe the electric generator under the following headings, (a) labelled diagram (b) working principle (c) working process

Ans-

(a) labelled diagram: -

(b) Principle : Electric generator works on the principle of electromagnetic induction. When a coil is rotated in a strong magnetic field, then the number of magnetic lines of force linked with the coil changes and an induced current starts flowing through the coil.
(c) Working:
The main parts of A.C. dynamo are: (i) magnet, (ii) Coil and crode, (iii) Rings.

Let initially the coil ABCD be in horizontal position. The moment it starts rotating arm AB moves up and CD goes down. Due to this induced current through the coil follows path ABCD and in the outer circuit path followed is S2B2B1S1. After half revolution side AB goes down and CD moves up, as a result of which the induced current reverses its direction. As the current reverses its direction after every half cycle, the current produced is called alternating current and the device is called A.C. generator.
Q. 14. Two circular side by side. If the direction of current through coil A be changed, will current induced in coil B ? Discuss with reason.

Ans. Two circular coils A and B are placed side by side. If current through coil A be changed, then current also flows through B which is similar to that flowing in A, because when current in any of the coupled coil is changed, the current starts flowing in the other coil due to induction.

Q. 15. Connect a coil of insulated copper wire with a galvanometer. What will happen if a bar magnet :

(a) be pushed into the coil, (b) be held stationary inside the coil, (c) be pulled outside from inside the coil?

Ans.

(a) In this case induced current will be developed in the coil.

(i)If north pole of magnet be pushed inside the coil then induced current will be anticlockwise.

(ii)If south pole is pushed inwards then induced current will be clockwise.

(b)No current will flow through the coil.

(c)If south pole is pulled outwards, current will be anticlockwise and for north pole, it will be clockwise.

Q. 16. State the law, which determines the direction of magnetic field developed around a straight conductor carrying current.

Ans.

Direction of magnetic field developed around a straight conductor carrying current is determined by Fleming's Right Hand Rule.

"According to this rule, if you place your right hand around the conductor in such a way that the thumb points towards the direction of current flow, then the fingers bent around the conductor will point in the direction of the lines of force, as shown in figure

Chapter -13

1. Choose the correct option:

1. Choose the correct option: (i) Concave lens is:
    - (a) Only diverging

(ii) If a mirror forms erect image for objects placed between pole and focus, and it forms Re al-Inverted image for object placed anywhere between focus and infinity, then the mirror is:

- (a) Concave

(iii) The image formed by convex mirror is always:

- (a) Smaller than object

(iv) The image formed by a convex lens is always:

- (d) smaller and real

(v) The focal length of a concave lens is 40 cm. For an object placed 40 cm away from the le ns, the image will be formed at:

- (b) 40 cm from lens on the opposite side

(vi) A lens is kept on the book and then raised by 3 cm. The text now appears erect and larg er. The focal length of lens is:

- (c) more than 3 cm

2. Fill in the blanks:

(i) The image formed by a convex mirror is always virtual and diminished, in all cases.
(ii) To obtain a real image of the same size as the object, from a convex lens, the object must be placed at twice the focal length (2F).
(iii) The power of a lens is +5.0 D. The focal length of the lens will be 20 cm.
(iv) The focal length of a convex lens is 25 cm. The power of this lens will be +4.0D

3. Write down the relation between radius of curvature and focal length of a spherical mirror.

The relationship between the radius of curvature (R) and the focal length (f) of a spherical mirror is given by the formula:

$$R=2f$$

This means that the radius of curvature is twice the focal length. This relationship holds true for both concave and convex mirrors

4. In what type(s) of mirrors is the linear magnification less than 1, equal to 1 or greater than 1.

Ans:- Concave Mirror:

- Less than 1: Object beyond center of curvature (C).
- Equal to 1: Object at center of curvature (C).
- Greater than 1: Object between center of curvature (C) and focal point (F).

Convex Mirror:

- Always less than 1.

Plane Mirror:

- Always equal to 1.

5. The rear-view mirrors used in vehicles are convex mirrors. Why?

Ans:-

Convex mirrors are used in rear-view mirrors because they provide a wider field of view compared to flat or concave mirrors. This allows drivers to see more of the area behind them, which is crucial for safe driving. Convex mirrors also produce smaller, upright images, which helps in judging the distance and speed of vehicles approaching from behind. This combination of a wider view and smaller images makes convex mirrors ideal for rear-view mirrors in vehicles.

6. If image is to be obtained on a screen, what type of mirror should be used?

Ans:-To obtain an image on a screen, you should use a concave mirror. Concave mirrors can produce real images, which can be projected onto a screen. These images are formed when the object is placed beyond the focal point of the mirror.

7. By drawing the ray diagrams for parallel incident beam of light, express what type of mirrors are converging & what type are diverging.

Ans:-

1. Converging Mirrors (Concave Mirrors):
    - When parallel rays of light fall on a concave mirror, they converge at a point called the focal point after reflection. This is because concave mirrors have a reflecting surface that curves inward, like the inside of a bowl.

2. Diverging Mirrors (Convex Mirrors):
    - When parallel rays of light fall on a convex mirror, they diverge after reflection. The reflected rays appear to come from a point behind the mirror called the focal point. Convex mirrors have a reflecting surface that curves outward, like the outside of a sphere.

8. Define the following for spherical mirrors: (i) Centre of curvature (ii) Radius of curvature (iii) Pole (iv) Aperture

Ans:-

1. Centre of Curvature: The center of the sphere from which the mirror is a part. For a concave mirror, it's located in front of the mirror, while for a convex mirror, it's behind the mirror.
2. Radius of Curvature: The distance between the center of curvature and the mirror's surface. It's essentially the radius of the sphere from which the mirror segment is taken.
3. Pole: The central point on the mirror's surface. It's the midpoint of the mirror.
4. Aperture: The diameter of the mirror's reflecting surface. It determines the size of the mirro

9. Write a note on the converging and diverging nature of lenses.

Ans:- Converging Lenses (Convex Lenses):

- Convex lenses are thicker in the middle and thinner at the edges.
- They cause parallel light rays to converge (come together) at a point known as the focal point.
- These lenses are used in applications like magnifying glasses, cameras, and corrective lenses for farsightedness.

Diverging Lenses (Concave Lenses):

- Concave lenses are thinner in the middle and thicker at the edges.
- They cause parallel light rays to diverge (spread apart) as if they are originating from a point known as the focal point.
- These lenses are used in applications like peepholes, laser beams, and corrective lenses for near sightedness.

10. What is power of a lens. Write its unit.

Ans:- The power of a lens measures its ability to converge or diverge light. It is defined as the reciprocal of the focal length (in meters) of the lens. Mathematically, it is expressed as:

$$P = \frac{1}{f}$$

where P is the power of the lens and f is the focal length in meters.The unit of power is the diopter (D). A lens with a focal length of 1 meter has a power of 1 diopter. Positive power indicates a converging lens (convex), while negative power indicates a diverging lens (concave).

11. Write down the sign convention used for lenses

Ans:-

1. Object Distance (u): Measured from the optical center of the lens. It is positive if the object is on the same side as the incoming light (usually the left side) and negative if on the opposite side.
2. Image Distance (v): Measured from the optical center of the lens. It is positive if the image is on the opposite side of the incoming light (usually the right side) and negative if on the same side.
3. Focal Length (f): Positive for convex (converging) lenses and negative for concave (diverging) lenses.
4. Height of Object (h_o) and Height of Image (h_i): Positive if measured upwards from the principal axis and negative if measured downwards.

12. What will be the power of a convex lens of focal length 50 cm? What if the lens is concave?

Ans:- To find the power of a lens, we use the formula:

$$P=1/f$$

where P is the power in diopters (D) and f is the focal length in meters.

For a convex lens with a focal length of 50 cm (0.5 meters):

$$P = \frac{1}{0.5} = 2\,D$$

So, the power of the convex lens is +2 diopters.

For a concave lens with the same focal length of 50 cm (0.5 meters), the focal length is considered negative:

$$P = \frac{1}{-0.5} = -2\,D$$

So, the power of the concave lens is -2 diopters.

13. An object is placed at 15 cm from the pole of a concave mirror of focal length 10 cm. What is the size, position, nature and magnification of the image?

Ans:- Let's calculate the image distance v:

$$\frac{1}{-10} = \frac{1}{v} + \frac{1}{-15}$$

$$\frac{1}{v} = \frac{1}{-15} + \frac{1}{10}$$

$$\frac{1}{v} = \frac{-3+2}{30}$$

$$\frac{1}{v} = \frac{1}{-30}$$

$$V = -30 \text{ cm}$$

So, the image distance v is -30 cm, meaning the image is formed 30 cm in front of the mirror.

Now, let's calculate the magnification mm:

$m = -\frac{v}{u}$

$m = -\frac{(-30)}{-15}$

$m = -2$

So, the magnification is 2, meaning the image is twice the size of the object.

Summary:

- Position: 30 cm in front of the mirror
- Size: Twice the size of the object
- Nature: Real and inverted
- Magnification: 2

14. The radius of curvature of a convex mirror is 30 cm. An object of height 5 cm is kept at a distance of 10 cm from the pole. Find the nature, size and magnification of image.

Ans:- The radius of curvature of a convex mirror is 30 cm. An object of height 5 cm is kept at a distance of 10 cm from the pole. Find the nature, size and magnification of image.

To find the nature, size, and magnification of the image formed by a convex mirror, we can use the mirror formula and magnification formula.

Let's calculate the image distance v:

$\frac{1}{15} = \frac{1}{v} + \frac{1}{-10}$

$\frac{1}{v} = \frac{1}{15} + \frac{1}{10}$

$\frac{1}{v} = \frac{12+3}{30}$

$\frac{1}{v} = \frac{5}{30}$

V = 6 cm

So, the image distance v is 6 cm, meaning the image is formed 6 cm behind the mirror.

Now, let's calculate the magnification mm:

$m = -\frac{v}{u}$

$m = -\frac{6}{-10}$

m= 0.6

m = 0.6

So, the magnification is 0.6, meaning the image is 0.6 times the size of the object.

Summary:

- Position: 6 cm behind the mirror
- Size: 0.6 times the size of the object (3 cm)
- Nature: Virtual and upright
- Magnification: 0.6

15. The focal length of a concave mirror is 10 cm. To obtain an image 5 times bigger than the object, where should the object be placed so that the image is (i) Real (ii) Virtual.

Ans:-

For a real image, the magnification m is 5:

$5 = -\frac{v}{u}$
$v = -5u$
v = -5u

Substitute vv in the mirror formula:

$\frac{1}{-10} = \frac{1}{-5u} + \frac{1}{u}$

$\frac{1}{-10} = -\frac{1}{5u} + \frac{1}{u}$

$\frac{1}{-10} = \frac{-1+5}{5u}$

$\frac{1}{-10} = \frac{4}{5u}$

$u = -8\text{cm}$

So, the object should be placed 8 cm in front of the mirror to obtain a real image 5 times bigger than the object.

16. The radius of curvature of a convex mirror is 30 cm. What will be the size, position and nature of the image if the object is placed at 12 cm from the pole. Do the same calculation for a concave mirror?

Ans:-

1. Convex Mirror:
    - Radius of Curvature (R): 30 cm
    - Focal Length (f): f=R/2=30/2=15 cm(positive for convex mirrors)
    - Object Distance (u): - 12 cm (negative as the object is in front of the mirror)

Using the mirror formula:

$$\frac{1}{f} = \frac{1}{v} + \frac{1}{u}$$

$$\frac{1}{15} = \frac{1}{v} + \frac{1}{-12}$$

$$\frac{1}{v} = \frac{1}{15} + \frac{1}{12}$$

$$\frac{1}{v} = \frac{4+5}{60}$$

$$\frac{1}{v} = \frac{9}{60}$$

$V = 60/9 \approx 6.67$ cm

So, the image distance v is approximately 6.67 cm behind the mirror.

Now, let's calculate the magnification mm:

$$m = -\frac{v}{u}$$

$$m = -\frac{6.67}{(-12)}$$

$m \approx 0.56m$

So, the magnification is approximately 0.56, meaning the image is 0.56 times the size of the object.

Summary for Convex Mirror:

- Position: 6.67 cm behind the mirror
- Size: 0.56 times the size of the object
- Nature: Virtual and upright

Now, let's do the same calculation for the concave mirror:

2. Concave Mirror:
    - Radius of Curvature (R): 30 cm
    - Focal Length (f): f=R / 2=30/2=15 (negative for concave mirrors)
    - Object Distance (u): -12 cm (negative as the object is in front of the mirror)

Using the mirror formula:

$$\frac{1}{f} = \frac{1}{v} + \frac{1}{u}$$

$$\frac{1}{-15} = \frac{1}{v} + \frac{1}{-12}$$

$$\frac{1}{v} = \frac{1}{-15} + \frac{1}{12}$$

$$\frac{1}{v} = \frac{-4+5}{60}$$

$$\frac{1}{v} = \frac{1}{60}$$

v = 60 cm

So, the image distance v is 60 cm in front of the mirror.

Now, let's calculate the magnification mm:

$$m = -\frac{v}{u}$$

$$m = -\frac{60}{(-12)}$$

$$m \approx 5m$$

So, the magnification is 5, meaning the image is 5 times the size of the object.

Summary for Concave Mirror:

- Position: 60 cm in front of the mirror
- Size: 5 times the size of the object
- Nature: Real and inverted

17. The image of an object kept at 30 cm from the pole of a convex mirror forms at 10 cm. What is the focal length of the mirror?

Ans:-

To find the focal length of the convex mirror, we can use the mirror formula:

$$\frac{1}{f} = \frac{1}{v} + \frac{1}{u}$$

So

$$\frac{1}{f} = \frac{1}{10} + \frac{1}{-30}$$

$$\frac{1}{f} = \frac{1}{10} - \frac{1}{30}$$

$$\frac{1}{f} = \frac{3-1}{30}$$

$$\frac{1}{f} = \frac{2}{30}$$

f =30 / 2

f =15 cm

So, the focal length of the convex mirror is 15 cm

18. he focal length of a concave mirror is 12 cm. If the object is placed at focus, where will the image be formed?

Ans:- When an object is placed at the focal point of a concave mirror, the reflected rays become parallel and do not converge to form an image. In this case, the image is formed at infinity. The image will be highly enlarged, real, and inverted.

19. The focal length of a convex lens is 15 cm. Where should be the object placed to obtain a Real image 3 times magnified

Ans:-

To obtain a real image that is 3 times magnified using a convex lens with a focal length of 15 cm, we can use the magnification formula and lens formula.

For a real image, the magnification m is - 3:

$$-3 = \frac{v}{u}$$

$$v = -3u$$

Substitute v in the lens formula:

$$\frac{1}{15} = \frac{1}{-3u} - \frac{1}{u}$$

$$\frac{1}{15} = \frac{-1-3}{3u}$$

$$\frac{1}{15} = \frac{-4}{3u}$$

$$u = \frac{-4}{3} \times 15$$

$$u = -20 \text{ cm}$$

So, the object should be placed 20 cm in front of the lens to obtain a real image that is 3 times magnified.

20. The focal length of a concave lens is 30 cm. What will be the position and size of the image if a 30 cm long object is placed at the focus

Ans:-

For a concave lens, when an object is placed at the focal point, the image formed is virtual, upright, and smaller than the object. Let's calculate the position and size of the image using the lens formula and magnification formula.

Let's calculate the image distance v:

$$\frac{1}{-30} = \frac{1}{v} - \frac{1}{-30}$$

$$\frac{1}{-30} = \frac{1}{v} + \frac{1}{30}$$

$$\frac{1}{v} = \frac{1}{-30} - \frac{1}{30}$$

$$\frac{1}{v} = \frac{-2}{30}$$

$$V = -15 \text{ cm}$$

So, the image distance v is -15 cm, meaning the image is formed 15 cm on the same side as the object.

Now, let's calculate the magnification mm:

$$m = \frac{v}{u}$$

$$m = \frac{-15}{-30}$$

$$m = 0.5$$

So, the magnification is 0.5, meaning the image is 0.5 times the size of the object.

Summary:

- Position: 15 cm on the same side as the object
- Size: 0.5 times the size of the object (15 cm)
- Nature: Virtual and upright

21. For an object kept at 30 cm from a concave lens, the magnification achieved in 2/3. What is the focal length of lens?

Ans:-

For an object kept at 30 cm from a concave lens, the magnification achieved in 2/3. What is the focal length of lens?

To find the focal length of the concave lens, we can use the magnification formula and lens)

Let's calculate the image distance v:

$$\frac{2}{3} = \frac{v}{-30}$$

v = −20 cm

Now, let's use the lens formula to find the focal length f:

$$\frac{1}{f} = \frac{1}{v} - \frac{1}{u}$$

$$\frac{1}{f} = \frac{1}{-20} - \frac{1}{-30}$$

$$\frac{1}{f} = \frac{-3+2}{60}$$

$$\frac{1}{f} = -\frac{-1}{60}$$

f = − 60 cm

22. For a convex lens of focal length 50 cm, what is the position of image if the object is placed at a distance of: (i) 25 cm, (ii) 75 cm , from the optical centre

Ans:-

(i) Object Distance (u) = 25 cm:

$$\frac{1}{50} = \frac{1}{v} - \frac{1}{(-25)}$$

$$\frac{1}{50} = \frac{1}{v} + \frac{1}{25}$$

$$\frac{1}{v} = \frac{1}{50} - \frac{1}{25}$$

$$\frac{1}{v} = \frac{1-2}{50}$$

$$\frac{1}{v} = \frac{-1}{50}$$

V = — 50 cm

(ii) Object Distance (u) = 75 cm:

$$\frac{1}{50} = \frac{1}{v} - \frac{1}{(-75)}$$

$$\frac{1}{50} = \frac{1}{v} + \frac{1}{75}$$

$$\frac{1}{v} = \frac{1}{50} - \frac{1}{75}$$

$$\frac{1}{v} = \frac{3-2}{150}$$

$$\frac{1}{v} = \frac{-1}{150}$$

v = — 150 cm

23. What is the focal length of a lens whose power is +1.5 D?

Ans:-

The power of a lens (P) is related to its focal length (f) by the formula:

$P = \frac{1}{f}$

where PP is the power in diopters (D) and ff is the focal length in meters.

Given the power P = +1.5D

$f = \frac{1}{P}$

f =11.5

f ≈ 0.67 meters

So, the focal length of the lens is approximately 0.67 meters (or 67 cm).

24. What is the power of a concave lens of focal length 20 cm? (

Ans:-

The power of a lens (P) is related to its focal length (f) by the formula:

$P = \frac{1}{f}$

where P is the power in diopters (D) and f is the focal length in meters.

Given the focal length f =−20 cm =− 0.2 meters (negative for concave lenses):

$P = \frac{1}{-0.2}$

P = −5 D

So, the power of the concave lens is -5 diopters.

Chapter -14

i) The following type of division takes place in most cells of our body:

- (d) mitosis

(ii) Which of the following is not a part of the female reproductive system:

- (c) sperm duct

(iii) Sexual reproduction leads to:

- (d) Both a and b

2. Is the placenta essential for the child developing in the uterus? Why?

Ans:- Yes, the placenta is essential for the developing child in the uterus. It acts as a lifeline between the mother and the fetus, providing oxygen and nutrients while removing waste products from the baby's blood. It also produces hormones that support pregnancy and protect the fetus from infections.

3.What is the role of male and female in the process of fertilization?

Ans;- In fertilization, the male's role is to produce and deliver sperm, which carries the genetic material. The female's role is to produce an egg (ovum) and provide a suitable environment for the sperm to reach and fertilize the egg. Once the sperm fertilizes the egg, it forms a zygote, which eventually develops into an embryo.

4.Draw a flower and label the male and female reproductive parts in it.

Ans:-

The male reproductive parts are the stamens, which consist of the anther (produces pollen) and filament.

- The female reproductive parts are the pistil, which includes the stigma (receives pollen), style, and ovary (contains ovules).

5. Five differences between asexual and sexual reproduction:

Ans:-

- Asexual reproduction involves a single parent, while sexual reproduction involves two parents.
- Asexual reproduction produces genetically identical offspring, while sexual reproduction produces genetically diverse offspring.
- Asexual reproduction is faster and simpler, while sexual reproduction is slower and more complex.
- Asexual reproduction occurs through processes like budding, fission, and vegetative propagation, while sexual reproduction involves the fusion of gametes.
- Asexual reproduction is common in unicellular organisms and some plants, while sexual reproduction is common in multicellular organisms, including animals and plants.

6. What is menstruation? What is its effect on the body of a human female? Menstruation is the monthly shedding of the uterine lining in females. It occurs when there is no fertilization of the egg. The effects on the body include hormonal changes, abdominal cramps, mood swings, and sometimes fatigue.

7. Two ways of contraception write in detail.

Ans:-

- Barrier Methods: These include condoms, diaphragms, and cervical caps, which physically prevent sperm from reaching the egg.
- Hormonal Methods: These include birth control pills, patches, and injections, which regulate or stop ovulation to prevent pregnancy.

8. Reproductive processes of unicellular and multicellular organisms write in detail.

Ans:-

- Unicellular Organisms: Reproduce mainly through asexual methods like binary fission (e.g., bacteria) and budding (e.g., yeast).
- Multicellular Organisms: Reproduce through both asexual methods (e.g., vegetative propagation in plants) and sexual methods (e.g., animals and flowering plants).

9. How does reproduction help in sustaining the population of a species?

Ans:- Reproduction ensures the continuation of a species by producing new individuals to replace those that die. It also introduces genetic variation, which helps populations adapt to changing environments and survive over time.

10. How do plants that do not produce seeds reproduce?

Ans:- Plants that do not produce seeds can reproduce through methods like vegetative propagation (e.g., runners in strawberries), spore formation (e.g., ferns), and budding (e.g., yeast).

Chapter -15

Assessment 1.

1. What do you think may have been the reason for Mendel's success?
    - (d) All above options
2. Mendel had studied certain contrasting characters of pea plants. Which character do you think was not chosen by Mendel?
    - (d) Round and wrinkled stem
3. If both of the parents can roll their tongue, what do you think would be the combinat ion of factors in them?
    - (b) Rr and Rr

Q-(2)Let us consider 4 major blood groups of humans A, B, AB and O. These had been named on the basis of certain antigenic factors.. The presence of both A and B factors represented AB blood type while absence of both represented O blood type. Let us take I to represent the substance responsible for the said factor. IO then represents absence of the substance. Now observe the following table and answer the questions given below the table.

• Those having blood group A would have how many IA factors?

Ans- at least one I A IS REQUIRED.

• Those of blood group O should have how many IO?

Ans- at least two IOIO required.

• Which factor do you think is recessive . IO, IA or IB?

Ans- IO is the recessive.

• 'A recessive character represents pure parental generation.' Justify this statement.

Ans-

Ans. Mendel from his experiment concluded that two alternative properties like-of the violet and white colour of the flowers one is dominating and other is recessive. Dominating property was called effective and recessive property he called ineffective because in the presence of dominating character the effect of the other is not observed. Among the colour of the flowers violet colour is effective and white is ineffective. If a seed has violet and white character then the colour of the flower is violet because violet colour dominates white. For white colour the property should be pure white. After performing these experiments in various generation he obtained a definite ratio in the number of pure and hybrid plants. By the conclusion of the above experiments of Mendel it is proved that "Ineffective or recessive factor always represent pure parental generation.

(v) Of the two children of the parent with blood group A, one child is of blood group O, then what will be the factors which represent the blood group of the parents ? What can be the blood group of the second child ?

Ans. If one child of the parent with blood group A has O blood group, then the factor representing the blood group of the parent will be IAIO, and the blood group of the other child will be A.

Q. 4. A breed of cow 'Jeba' is adapted for surviving in summer. Another breed of it Sahiwal gives about 20,000 litre of milk in a year. Body of another breed Angus is strong. To obtain maximum milk from a cow in Chhattisgarh, it should be hybridized with which of the cows and why ?

Ans. Of the three breeds of cow given here, the breed Sahiwal gives the maximum milk. Thus, in Chhattisgarh to obtain maximum milk from a cow, it should be hybridized with Sahiwal, because maximum milk is obtained from the breed Sahiwal.

Q. 5. How can the study of heredity help us for increasing the crop production ?
Ans. By the study of heredity, we have come to know that by the hybridization of plants of different characters of a species seeds of desired characters can be obtained and by the seed obtained production of crops can be increased. This way, study of heredity can help us for increasing the crop production.

Q. 6. How can we obtain a new variety of plants by the selection of characters ?

Ans. In his experiment Mendel sowed seeds of different characters of two plants of pure violet and pure white flowers and cross-pollinated them. This way, the hybrid seed formed when sown produced plants with violet flowers. By repeating this experiment for several generation he obtained a definite ratio between pure and hybrid plant and obtained a new variety of plant in each generation. This way, by following the above method of Mendel, we can also select two plants of different characters and hyridize them to obtain a new variety of plants.
Q. 7. A farmer sowed seeds of pea plant of violet flowers and emphasized that plants of violet flowers will be obtained in the next generation. Was he correct ?
Ans. Yes, the farmer was correct, because by following the experiment of Mendel, the farmer performed self-pollination in the pea plant of violet flowers and obtained such violet flowers plants which showed their characteristics generarion after generartion. Thus, in the next generation by violet flower pea plants, plants of violet flower only will be obtained.

Q. 8. We have been able to successfully obtain pink flowered Rose plants by crossing white and red coloured Rose plants respectively. .Do you think that some characters do intermix? Why? Site some other examples of this type that are related to agriculture.
Ans.

In the properties of opposite pairs, one character is not completely effective over the other. Plants or Red flower of Mirabilis jalapa is crossed with plants of white flower then in the first generation pink colour flowers are obtained. In the second generation (F2) phenotype ratio is 1 : 2 : 1.
In the above experiment Rr factor intermix
Other such examples related to agriculture : By cross breeding (hybridizing) paddy and wheat plants of different character of the same species, seed of desired characters can be obtained.

Q.9.What would happen if you played the game of coins with just one coin? What is the probability of getting a head then?
Ans.
(a) If we play with only one coin, then the possibility of the front and back side is 1/2.
(b) On throwing two coins together in one time four situations are obtained in both the coins (HH, HT, TH, TT) and their ratio obtained is 1: 1 : 1 : 1.
Thus, each time the situation obtained is 25 percent.
Q. 10.Can we develop high yielding variety seeds by hybridization? Can such seeds be developed only by crossing pure varieties?

Ans. On the basis of knowledge of the factors, we can ourselves prepare high quality seeds. For this, we have to select two different variety plants and hybridize them to obtain hybrid seeds.

Q-11) The sweetness of milk is due to the presence of Lactose (a type of sugar) in it. You may have heard about people who fail to digest milk and milk products. The factor responsible for the production of the enzyme capable of digesting lactose is usually not present in these people. Even if a single factor for formation of the enzyme is present, lactose digesting enzyme is formed. Now answer the following questions on the basis of this information-

• What would be the combination of factors of a child who fails to digest milk and milk products? What are characters represented by such factors called?

Ans-

If mother and father can digest milk and the child cannot, then the factor of such motherfather will be L and L.

• What is the combination of factors in the parents of such a child(take a lactose digesting factor as L)who are capable of digesting milk?

Ans- Factors of the child will be LL (where L is not digesting factor) such pairs of factors are called hetero form factors.

• What percent of children of such parents would be able to digest milk?

Ans-

75% children of these parents will digest milk.

Q-12. In green gram, the development of two flowers at the axial position is a recessive character, while the development of a single flower at the axial position is a dominant character. If the dominant condition is represented by 'SS' and recessive by 'ss' then answer the following questions -

• Find out the percentages of pure and hybrid plants obtained in the second generation(F2 generation) after crossing pure parental varieties.

Ans-

On cross pollinating pure effective plants SS and pure ineffective plants ss. Plants of first generation be heteroform monoflowering plants Ss pairs of factors will be formed this way.

	S	S
s	Ss	Ss
s	Ss	Ss

Ovary and pollen grain of the second generation will be as follows :

(S) (s) (S) (s)

Pairs of factors of the second generation will be performed as follows :

	S	s
S	Ss	Ss
s	Ss	ss

On the basis of the above table, percentage of monoflowering plants of the second generation is 25% and biflowering plants is 25%.

• Find out the percentage of each variety of offsprings obtained by a cross between Heterozygous Ss and pure ss varieties.

Ans-

Pairs of factors of heteroform monoflowering plant Ss and pure ineffective flowering plants ss is as follows :

	S	s
s	Ss	ss
s	Ss	ss

On the basis of the above table percentage of mono-flowering plants is zero per cent and bi-flowering plants is 50%.

• What would be the percentage of varieties with single axial flowers when a cross between homozygous variety SS and heterozygous variety Ss is conducted?

Ans-

On cross breeding pure effective mono flowering plants SS and heteroform mono-flowering plants Ss pairs of factors will be as follows :

	S	S
S	SS	SS
s	Ss	Ss

On the basis of the above table percentage of mono-flowering plants is 50%.

Chapter -16

Internal questions (Page -272)

1. Identify and write the names of the functional groups in the following compounds C_3H_7OH, C_4H_9Cl, CH_3CHO, $C_5H_{11}COOH$

Ans:- C_3H_7OH: The functional group is hydroxyl (-OH), which classifies it as an alcohol.

C_4H_9Cl: The functional group is chloro (-Cl), which classifies it as an alkyl halide.

CH_3CHO: The functional group is aldehyde (-CHO), which classifies it as an aldehyde.

$C_5H_{11}COOH$: The functional group is carboxyl (-COOH), which classifies it as a carboxylic acid.

2. Write the names of the compounds formed by joining –OH functional group to ethyl and propyl groups respectively.

Ans:- the names of the compounds formed by joining the –OH functional group to ethyl and propyl groups:

1. Ethyl group + –OH: Ethanol (C_2H_5OH)
2. Propyl group + –OH: Propanol (C_3H_7OH)

3. Name the compounds formed when –Br and –COOH are added to methyl groups.

Ans:- the names of the compounds formed when –Br and –COOH are added to mcthyl groups:

1. Methyl group + –Br: Bromoethane (CH_3Br)
2. Methyl group + –COOH: Acetic acid (CH_3COOH)

4.Write the names of two compounds having hydroxyl group and two having hydroxide group.

Ans:- Compounds with Hydroxyl Group (-OH):

1. Ethanol (C_2H_5OH)
2. Methanol (CH_3OH)

Compounds with Hydroxide Group (OH-):

1. Sodium hydroxide (NaOH)
2. Potassium hydroxide (KOH)

5. Write the IUPAC name of the given compound.

Ans:- 2-Butanol (sec-Butanol): The hydroxyl group (-OH) is attached to the second carbon atom.

6. Write the structural formula of 2–methylpropan–1–ol.

```
Ans:-      H   H   H
           |   |   |
       H — C — C — C — OH
           |   |   |
           H  CH3  H
```

7. structural formulae of all possible isomers of C_3H_8O.

Ans:- 1. 1-Propanol

2.2-Propanol

3. Methoxyethane

Internal question (Page-272)

1. What are molasses?

   Ans:- Industrial manufacture of ethanol (ethyl alcohol) is done using fermentation method. In this process, sugar is first separated from cane–sugar juice by crystallization. The thick, yellow syrupy substance left behind is called molasses.

2. What will happen when:

(a) Ethanol is heated in the presence of concentrated sulphuric acid.

Ans:- When ethanol is heated in the presence of concentrated sulphuric acid, it undergoes a dehydration reaction to form ethylene (ethene). The reaction can be represented as:

$$C_2H_5OH \xrightarrow{H_2SO_4} C_2H_4 + H_2O$$

(b) Yeast is added to molasses

Ans:- When yeast is added to molasses, the yeast ferments the sugars present in the molasses to produce ethanol and carbon dioxide. This process is known as fermentation.

Page-278

1. Write the structures of all possible isomers of $C_6H_{12}O_2$

   Ans:-

1. Hexanoic acid:

```
     H  H  H  H  H  H
     |  |  |  |  |  |
   H—C—C—C—C—C—C—OH
     |  |  |  |  |  |
     H  H  H  H  H  H
```

2. 3-Methylbutanoic acid:

```
     H  H  H  H
     |  |  |  |
   H—C—C—C—C—OH
     |  |  |  |
     H  H  H  H
```

3. What is the IUPAC name of formic acid?
Ans:- . The IUPAC name of formic acid is methanoic acid.

Exercise

Multiple choice question: -

(i) When ethanol has 5% water added to it, it is called:

- (a) Rectified spirit

(ii) Packing gasket is made of:

- (c) Teflon

(iii) If sodium carbonate is added to ethanoic acid, a gas is evolved with rapid bubbling. This gas is:

- (b) CO2

(iv) The IUPAC name of acetic acid is:

- (a) Ethanoic acid

2. What happens when-
   (i) Ethanoic acid reacts with sodium
   (ii) Ethanol reacts with sodium
   Ans:-

(i) Ethanoic acid reacts with sodium: When ethanoic acid (acetic acid) reacts with sodium, it produces sodium acetate and hydrogen gas. The reaction can be represented as:
$2CH_3COOH+2Na \rightarrow 2CH_3COONa+H_2$

(ii) Ethanol reacts with sodium: When ethanol reacts with sodium, it produces sodium ethoxide and hydrogen gas. The reaction can be represented as:
$2C_2H_5OH+2Na \rightarrow 2C_2H_5ONa+H_2$

3. Complete the following chemical eqautions:
(i) $C_2H_5COOH + ? \rightarrow (C_2H_5COO)\ 2Mg + H_2$
(ii) $CH_3OH + CH_3COOH \rightarrow ? + H_2O$
(iii) $CH_3COOH + Na_2CO_3 \rightarrow\ ? + ? + CO_2$

Ans:- the completed chemical equations:
(i) $C_2H_5COOH + Mg \rightarrow (C_2H_5COO)_2Mg + H_2$
(ii) $CH_3OH + CH_3COOH \rightarrow CH_3COOCH_3 + H_2O$
(iii) $CH_3COOH + Na_2CO_3 \rightarrow 2CH_3COONa + H_2O + CO_2$

3. Why is ethanol used in thermometers?
   Ans:-
   Ethanol is used in thermometers because it has a low freezing point (-114°C) and a high boiling point (78°C), making it suitable for measuring a wide range of temperatures. It's also less toxic than mercury and has good thermal expansion

properties, which means it expands and contracts uniformly with temperature changes.

4. How is ethene obtained from ethanol?

Ans:-

Ethene (ethylene) is obtained from ethanol through a dehydration reaction. When ethanol is heated in the presence of concentrated sulfuric acid (H2SO4), it undergoes dehydration to form ethene and water. The reaction can be represented as:

$$C_2H_5OH \xrightarrow{H_2SO_4} C_2H_4 + H_2O$$

5. Structures of possible isomers of $C_5H_{10}O_2$:

Here are the structures of some possible isomers of $C_5H_{10}O_2$:

1. Pentanoic acid (Valeric acid):

```
     H H  H  H   H
     |  |   |   |   |
H—C—C—C—C—C—OH
     |  |   |   |   |
     H  H H  H  H
```

2. Methyl butanoate:

```
     H   H  H  H
     |   |   |   |
H—C—C—C—C—O—C—H
     |  |      |  |
     H H    H  H
```

3. Ethyl propanoate:

```
     H  H  H
     |   |   |
H—C—C—C—O—C—C—H
     |   |   |
     H  H  H
```

4. 2-Methylbutanoic acid:

```
     H   H   H H
     |   |   |   |
H—C—C—C—C—OH
     |   |   |   |
     H   H  H   H
```

6. How is ethanol manufactured industrially?

Ans:- Ethanol is manufactured industrially through two main processes:

- Fermentation: Sugars from crops like corn, sugarcane, or wheat are fermented by yeast to produce ethanol and carbon dioxide.

- Hydration of Ethene: Ethene is reacted with water in the presence of a catalyst (usually phosphoric acid) to produce ethanol.

7. What is vinegar? How is it manufactured?
   Ans:-
   Vinegar is a solution of acetic acid (CH_3COOH) in water, typically containing 4-8% acetic acid by volume. It is manufactured through the fermentation of ethanol by acetic acid bacteria. The process involves two steps:

- Alcoholic Fermentation: Yeast converts sugars into ethanol.
- Acetic Acid Fermentation: Acetic acid bacteria oxidize ethanol to acetic acid.

9. Condensed structure of PVC and its uses: The condensed structure of Polyvinyl Chloride (PVC) is:

$$[-CH_2\text{-}CHCl\text{-}]_n$$

Uses of PVC:

1. Pipes and fittings: Widely used in plumbing and drainage systems.
2. Electrical insulation: Used for insulating electrical cables.
3. Construction materials: Used in window frames, doors, and flooring.
4. Medical devices

13. What is a polymer? Explain the polymerization of ethene.

Ans:- A polymer is a large molecule composed of repeating structural units called monomers, which are covalently bonded together. Polymers can be natural (like DNA, proteins) or synthetic (like plastics).

Polymerization of Ethene: Ethene (ethylene) undergoes addition polymerization to form polyethene (polyethylene). In this process, ethene molecules (C2H4) react under high pressure and temperature in the presence of a catalyst to form long chains of polyethene. The reaction can be represented as:
$nC_2H_4 \rightarrow (C_2H_4)n$

14. Difference between Low Density Polythene (LDPE) and High Density Polythene (HDPE):

- LDPE:
  - Structure: Branched polymer chains.
  - Density: Lower density.
  - Properties: Flexible, less crystalline, lower melting point.
  - Uses: Plastic bags, squeeze bottles, insulation for electrical wires.
- HDPE:
  - Structure: Linear polymer chains.
  - Density: Higher density.

- Properties: Rigid, more crystalline, higher melting point.
- Uses: Milk jugs, detergent bottles, water pipes, plastic lumber.

15. Identifying Compounds A and B:

- Compound A: Ethanol (C_2H_5OH) with a molecular weight of 46u, used as a sterilizing agent.
- Compound B: Acetic acid (CH_3COOH) formed by the oxidation of ethanol.

Balanced Chemical Equation:
$C_2H_5OH + O_2 \rightarrow CH_3COOH + H_2O$

Chapter -17

Internal question

Q-1. We have two water samples, 'A' and 'B'. Sodium hydrogen carbonate was found in sample 'A' and magnesium sulphate was found in sample 'B'. Which sample of water is hard and why?

Ans-

Sample B is hard water. : This is because of the presence of dissolved salts of calcium or magnesium chlorides and/or calcium and magnesium sulphates in water. Permanent hardness cannot be removed by boiling or treatment with limewater.

Q-2) Give two natural sources of common salt.
Ans-
salt mines, sea water
Q3) Write the chemical formula and two important uses of baking soda.
Ans-
Baking soda is often used in the kitchen to obtain spongy cakes and breads. it is also used to cook food faster. Its chemical name is sodium hydrogen carbonate and it is also known as sodium bicarbonate.
Baking soda is produced by Solvay ammonia process which uses salt as one of the raw materials.

$NaCl + H_2O + CO_2 + NH_3 \rightarrow NH_4Cl + NaHCO_3$

Ammonium chloride   sodium hydrogen carbonate

Use of baking soda-

1)Sodium hydrogen carbonate is used as an antacid to reduce acidity of stomachs. Being alkaline, it neutralizes excess acid in the stomach.

2). Baking soda is also used in soda-acid fire extinguishers.

Q-4) What is efflorescence?

Ans-

The chemical formula of washing soda is $Na_2CO_3 .10H_2O$. 10 molecules of water are attached to each molecule of crystalline sodium carbonate. Washing soda is a white-coloured crystalline solid with attached water molecules. Water of crystallization is the fixed number of water molecules present in one formula unit of a salt. When washing soda is left in open air, it loses nine water molecules and gets converted into a white powder of sodium carbonate monohydrate. This property is known as efflorescence.

$$Na_2CO_3 .10H_2O(s) \rightarrow Na_2CO_3 .H_2O(s) + 9H_2O$$

left in open

Q-5) Baking powder is a mixture of which two compounds?
Ans-
Baking powder is a mixture of baking soda and tartaric acid.

Q-6) Which property of Plaster of Paris is the reason why doctors use it in setting fractures?

Ans-

Plaster of Paris is a white powder and on mixing with water, it changes once again to gypsum giving a hard solid mass.

$$CaSO_4 . \frac{1}{2} H_2O \quad + \quad 1\frac{1}{2} H_2O \quad \rightarrow \quad CaSO_4 . 2H_2O$$

It is used by doctors for supporting fractured bones in the right position.

Q-7) Name the substance that reacts with chlorine to give bleaching powder.
Ans-
Bleaching powder is produced by the action of chlorine gas on dry slaked lime.

bleaching powder is known as calcium oxychloride ($CaOCl_2$).

$$Ca(OH)_2(s) + Cl_2(g) \quad \rightarrow \quad CaOCl_2(s) + H_2O(g)$$

Q-8) Why is gypsum added to cement?
Ans-
When cement is mixed with sand and water and left for some time, it sets and becomes as hard as a rock. Gypsum is added to cement to slow down the setting process.

Q-9) Why are cullet's used in glass manufacture?
Ans-

Cullet is defined as recycled broken or waste glass used in glassmaking, and furnace-ready cullet is uniform in size, free of contaminants and often sorted by color. Cullet creation is the form of glass recycling that saves huge quantities of energy and toxic emissions.

Q-10) The melting point of glass is not fixed, why?
Ans-
Glass is a mixture of silica and metal silicates. It is non-crystalline, hard, brittle, and transparent and appears solid. And there are no consistent distances between the bonded particles, they break up at different temperatures. This results in glass not having a specific, fixed melting point. The general formula of glass is: $xR_2O.yMO.6SiO_2$

Q-11) Can you use detergents to determine if a given sample of water is hard or not?

Ans-

No we cannot because detergents are effective even in case of hard water. They can clean clothes and make bubbles.

Q-12) When washing clothes, after applying soap we either scrub with a brush or beat clothes over a stone or beat them with a stick. Why do we need to scrub clothes to clean them?

Ans-

When clothes are soaked in soap solution, then the negatively charged part of soap surrounds the oil (dirt). A sphere is formed around the oil drop in such a way that the end with the hydrocarbon chain (tail) is inside the sphere and the COO– end is on the outer part of the sphere. Thus, the soap molecules form micelles. The micelles get distributed in water forming a colloid which is removed when we rub the cloth and rinse with water.

Exercise question

1. Choose the correct option

(i) The chemical formula of baking soda is:

(a) $NaHSO_4$ (b) Na_2CO_3 (c) $NaHCO_3$ (d) $Na_2CO_3 .10H_2O$

(ii) The chemical substance that is used for disinfecting drinking water to make it free of germs is:

(a) $CaCl_2$ (b) $CaOCl_2$ (c) $FeCl_3$ (d) $MgCl_2$

(iii) Glass is a

(a) Liquid (b) Solid (c) Transparent carbon polymer (d) Super-cooled liquid

(iv) Plaster of Paris hardens by

(a) Losing $CaCl_2$ (b) Releasing CO_2 (c) Absorbing water (d) Releasing water

Q-3.) What is hard water? What is soft water?

Ans:-

Water is called hard water or soft water depending on the amount of salts present in it and also on how much lather it produces with soap.

- Hard Water:

It takes a long time to form lather with soap and very little lather is seen. Instead, hard water forms a precipitate, known as soap scum, with soap.

- Soft water:

It quickly forms a lot of lather with soap. Rain water and distilled water are two examples of soft water.

Q-4) What are the factors that cause hardness of water? How many types of hardness are there?

Ans-

The presence of dissolved salts of magnesium or calcium causes hardness of water. The salts can be hydrogen carbonates or sulphates or carbonates.

Types of hardness: -

(1) Temporary hardness: This is caused if dissolved calcium or magnesium hydrogen carbonates are present in water. It can be removed by boiling.

$$Ca(HCO_3)_{2}(aq) \xrightarrow{\text{Boiling}} CaCO_3 + H_2O + CO_2$$

(2) Permanent hardness: This is caused by the presence of dissolved salts of calcium or magnesium chlorides and/or calcium and magnesium sulphates in water. Permanent hardness cannot be removed by boiling or treatment with limewater.

Q-5) How do animals and plants, living in lakes and ponds in snowy regions, survive during winter?

Ans-

During winter months in colder countries the outside or atmospheric temperature is very low – it drops to below freezing – and the upper layers of water in the lakes and ponds start cooling. The light frozen layer of ice floats on top.Ice does not allow heat to pass through it easily, so the freezing of the waters below is a very slow process. As a result animals have adapted to this situation by growing more slowly.

Q-6)What is baking powder? How does it make cakes soft and spongy?

Ans-

– Baking powder is a mixture of baking soda and tartaric acid. When baking powder is heated or mixed with water, the following reaction takes place–

$NaHCO_3 + H^+$ (from acid) -----> CO_2 + H_2O + Sodium salt of acid (from acid)

Carbon dioxide produced during the reaction causes bread or cakes to rise, making them soft and spongy.

Q-7) What is the process of making Plaster of Paris? Why is it stored in air-tight containers?

Ans-

Chemically, Plaster of Paris is calcium sulphate hemihydrate. Its chemical formula is

. $CaSO_4 .½H_2O$ or $(CaSO_4)$ 2 H_2O .

It is formed by heating gypsum at 100°C.

$CaSO_4 .2H_2O$ 100°C > $CaSO_4 .½H2O$ + 1½H_2O

gypsum Plaster of Paris Plaster of Paris is a white powder and on mixing with water, It is contained in air tight container because it changes once again to gypsum giving a hard solid mass When it comes with contact of water or moist air present in the atmosphere.

$CaSO_4 .½ H_2O$ + 1½ H_2O $CaSO_4 .2H_2O$

Q-8) What is the chemical name for washing soda? Name the three main raw materials used to produce washing soda by the Solvay ammonia process.

Ans-

The chemical name of washing soda is sodium carbonate ($Na_2CO_3 .10H_2O$). the three main raw materials used to produce washing soda by the Solvay ammonia process are sodium chloride(NaCl) and calcium carbonate ($CaCO_3$). And ammonia(NH_3).

Q-9) A compound of calcium, which is a white powder having a yellow tinge, is used in the textile industry and as a disinfectant.

(i) Name the compound.

(ii) Which gas is released when the compound is left out in open air? Give the balanced equation for this reaction.

Ans-

A compound of calcium, which is a white powder having a yellow tinge, is used in the textile industry and as a disinfectant. Is

(i) Bleaching powder ,It is also referred to as chloride of lime.

(ii) It is a white powder having a yellowish tinge with a strong smell of chlorine.

When left in the open, it reacts with carbon dioxide to release chlorine gas.

$CaOCl_2(s) + CO_2(g)$ -----> $CaCO_3(s) + Cl_2(g)$

Q-10). A compound of sodium, 'X', is a white powder and an important component of baking powder. When 'X' is heated, a gas 'Y' is produced that turns lime water milky.

(i) Write the chemical equation for the reaction which takes place on heating.

(ii) Why is 'X' used as an antacid?

Ans-

A compound of sodium, 'X', is a white powder and an important component of baking powder is baking soda (sodium hydrogen carbonet).
(i)When sodium hydrogencarbonate is heated it decomposes to form sodium carbonate with production of carbon dioxide gas.

$$2NaHCO_3 \xrightarrow{\text{(Heat)}} Na_2CO_3 + H_2O + CO_2$$

sodium carbonate

(ii) Sodium hydrogen carbonate is used as an antacid to reduce acidity of stomachs. Being alkaline, it neutralizes excess acid in the stomach.

Q-11) Describe the steps in the process of glass manufacture under each of the following headings:
(i) Necessary materials

(ii) Substances that give or impart colour to glass

(iii) The chemical reaction taking place in tank furnace

Ans-

(i)The materials used in manufacture of glass are:

1. Silica: in the form of sand.

2. Alkali metal: in the form of sodium carbonate or potassium carbonate or mixture of salt cake and carbon (Na_2SO_4 + C).

3. Divalent metal: such as calcium in the form of limestone or lead in the form of litharge (PbO) or red lead oxide (Pb_3O_4).

4. Oxidizing agents or materials to remove colour (bleaching agents): manganese dioxide (MnO2), potassium nitrate (KNO_3) or sodium nitrate ($NaNO_3$).

5. Cullet's: pieces of broken glass

(ii)Colouring materials: Various compounds used to impart different colours to glass

Colour of glass	Colouring material

Green	chromium oxide
Yellow	cadmium sulphide
Red	copper oxide
Purple	manganese oxide
Blue	cobalt oxide

(iii) The chemical reaction taking place in tank furnace-

$$Na_2CO3 + SiO_2 \rightarrow Na_2SiO_3 + CO_2 \uparrow$$

$$CaCO_3 + SiO_2 \rightarrow CaSiO_3 + CO_2 \uparrow$$

$$Na_2SiO_3 + CaSiO_3 + 4SiO_2 \rightarrow Na_2O.CaO.6SiO_2$$

(glass)

Q-12. Write the different steps involved in cement production.

Ans-

Cement manufacture: -

The raw materials needed in manufacture of cement are limestone (CaCO3), clay and gypsum. Clay contains large quantities of oxides of iron, aluminium and silicon. The steps in cement production are as follows:

(i) Three parts limestone and one-part clay are pulverized to fine powder separately. The powders are mixed and heated in a kiln where temperature is maintained between 1100-1800°C

(ii) At 1100°C, limestone undergoes thermal decomposition and forms calcium oxide.

$$CaCO_3 \xrightarrow{1100°C} CaO + CO_2$$

(iii) Calcium oxide reacts with the other oxides present in clay.

$$2CaO + SiO_2 \xrightarrow{1400\text{-}1500°C} 2CaO.SiO_2$$

Dicalcium silicate

$3CaO + SiO_2$ ----1400-1500°C-------> $3CaO.SiO2$

Tricalcium silicate

$3CaO + Al_2O_3$ ----1400-1500°C--------> $3CaO.Al_2O_3$

Tricalcium aluminate

$4CaO + Al_2O_3 + Fe_2O_3$ -----above 1500°C -------> $4CaO.Al_2O_3.Fe_2O_3$

Tetracalcium alumino ferrite

(iv) The aluminate and silicate mixture obtained from the furnace is in the form of small, hard balls or pebbles and is called clinker.

(v) Clinker is cooled and 2-3% gypsum ($CaSO_4.2H_2O$) is added to it. This mixture is pulverized into a fine powder.

Flowchart:-

Limestone + Clay

↓ Mixed in correct proportion & pulverized

Rotary kiln

↓ Heated

Clinker

↓ Cooled

2-3% Gypsum

↓ Added

Ball mill

↓ Pulverized

Cement

Q-13)How are soap-micelles formed? Describe.

Ans-

The molecules of soap are sodium or potassium salts of long chain carboxylic acids and are denoted by RCOOM. When soap is dissolved in water, it ionizes into RCOO– and metal, M+ ions. The RCOO– ion has two parts. One is R which is a long hydrocarbon chain that forms the tail of the carboxylate ion and gets attached to the oil molecules. The second part is COO– which forms the head and is soluble in water.

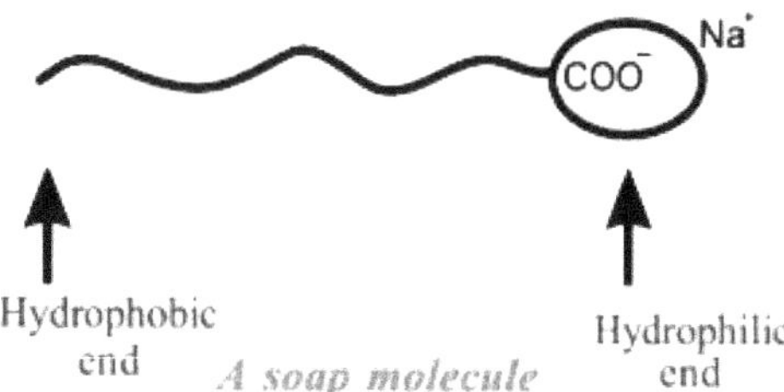

A soap molecule

When clothes are soaked in soap solution, then the negatively charged part of soap surrounds the oil (dirt). A sphere is formed around the oil drop in such a way that the end with the hydrocarbon chain (tail) is inside the sphere and the COO– end is on the outer part of the sphere. Thus, the soap molecules form micelles.

The micelles get distributed in water forming a colloid which is removed when we rub the cloth and rinse with water

Chapter -18

1. Choose the correct option:

1.
2. Most of the energy sources used by us utilize solar energy. Which energy source out of following is not derived from solar energy:
    - (a) Geo thermal energy
3. Biogas is a mixture of following gases:
    - (d) Methane, Carbon dioxide, Hydrogen
4. Nuclear fission is a reaction in which:
    - (b) Breaking of a heavy nucleus into light nuclei.
5. Fossil fuels are:
    - (a) Coal, petroleum, natural gas
6. Solar cell is a device which converts:
    -

2. Fill in the blanks-

(i) We cannot use solar heaters on a .rainy. day to heat water.
(ii) Lighting a torch is conversion of chemical energy into heat energy.
(iii) The energy generated due to oceans is tidal energy,
(iv) A solar cooker converts solar energy into thermal energy.
3.Explain the mechanism of solar cooker with the help of a labelled diagram,
Ans-Solar cooker: Solar cooker is a device which is used to cook food using the radiation heat energy of the sun
Diag:-

A box-type solar cooker consists of the following components:
Black Box – The box is an insulated metal or wooden box which is painted black from the inside to absorb more heat.
Glass Cover – A cover made of two sheets of toughened glass held together in an aluminium frame is used as a cover for box.
Plane Mirror reflector – The plane mirror reflector is fixed to box B with the help of hinges. The mirror reflector can be positioned at any desired angle to the box. The mirror is positioned so as to allow the reflected sunlight to fall on the glass cover of the box.
Cooking Containers – A set of aluminium containers blackened from the outside are kept in box.
Working: -
Solar cooker placed under the sun so that maximum rays fall on it. Once the heat waves of sun enter the box, the glass cover does not allow them to escape out of box easily. This way, maximum energy of the heat waves is captured inside the box due to which the temperature of solar cooker box increases to 100-140° C in 2-3 hours. This heat is used to cook edible foods like, rice, pulses and vegetables inside the black pots
4. Explain why-
(i) The inside of a solar cooker box is painted black.
Ans-
The inside of a solar cooker box is painted black because black colour absorbs all radiation from the sun and heat inside the box raises rapidly and food get cooked.
(ii) The solar cooker box is covered with a glass-sheet.
Ans-
inside the jar the heat that is generated from the sunlight energy is unable to escape—glass does not allow heat radiation to pass through. Because the heated air inside the jar is trapped, there is also no airflow possible. This means the warm air cannot mix with colder air to cool it down. That's why The solar cooker box is covered with a glass-sheet.

(iii) Plane mirror reflectors are used inside the solar cookers
Ans-
In solar cooker in order to generate heat in large amounts, you need sufficient sunlight. So, to concentrate the light coming from the sun in the direction where the cooking substance is placed. It is known as the cooking space. To achieve this, plane mirrors are used to concentrate the sunlight. Sufficient amounts can be concentrated by reflecting sunlight on a plane mirror.
5. Name the device which converts solar energy into electric energy.
Ans-
A solar cell is an electrical device that converts the energy of light directly into electricity by the photovoltaic effect, which is a physical and chemical phenomenon. A typical cell develops a voltage of 0.5-1 V and can produce about 0.7 W of electricity when exposed to

the Sun. A large number of solar cells are, combined in an arrangement called solar cell panel that can deliver enough electricity for practical use.

6. Apart from cattle-dung, which other material can be put inside a biogas plant?
Ans-
Apart from cattle-dung, various plant materials like the residue after harvesting the crops, vegetable waste and sewage etc could be used for biogas plant.
7. Explain any two differences between nuclear fusion and nuclear fission.
Ans-

Nuclear fission	Nuclear fusion
1.Nuclear fission is a reaction the nucleus of a heavy atom (such as uranium, plutonium or thorium), when bombarded with low-energy neutrons, can be split apart into lighter nuclei. 2) it is controlled chain reaction.	1) nuclear fusion. Fusion means joining lighter nuclei to make a heavier nucleus,It takes considerable energy to force the nuclei to fuse. 2) it is an un-controlled reaction
3). The fission of an atom of uranium, for example, produces 10 million times the energy produced by the combustion of an atom of carbon from coal.	3)It releases a tremendous amount of energy more than nuclear fission, The conditions needed for this process are extreme - millions of degrees of temperature and millions of Pascal's of pressure.

8. On what basis we can classify the sources of energy into renewable and non-renewable.
Ans-
The basis for the classification of energy into renewable and non-renewable energy is whether the energy sources can be replenished easily or not and whether it is present in a limited amount in nature or abundantly in nature.
Renewable- those energy sources which are abundant in nature and can be easily replenished are called renewable energy sources. Renewable energy sources like- wind energy, water energy, solar energy, ocean energy, thermal energy etc. also called non-conventional energy.

Non-renewable - Those energy sources which are limited in nature and cannot be replenished easily are called non-renewable energy sources. Non-renewable sources like- coal, petroleum, wood, natural gas, etc. Also called conventional energy sources.

9. Write two sources of energy which you think are renewable. Give reasons for your choices.
Ans-
Two sources of energy are-
1.wind energy 2. Solar energy
Reasons-
These two energy sources are renewable sources because both are in abundant in nature and they can replenish regularly in case of solar energy it is continuously present in nature. So we can use them again and again.
10. Write down the benefits of use of solar energy.
Ans-
Solar energy is the enrgy that we get from the sun and some benefits of using solar energy are-
1)it is present in nature abundantly, which means it can be used many time as we want.
2)it is clean source of energy it doesn't give any by-product. Like- smoke, sound etc.
3)it can be directly converted to electric energy.

11. What are limitations of wind energy?
Ans-
The wind mill harnesses the wind energy but there are some limitations to wind energy-
1.wind of particular speed is needed otherwise it won't be able to generate electricity.
2.its energy is totally dependent on wind and if enough wind is not present then required electricity could not be achieved from it.
3.. Windmills are placed in such area where continuous wind is blowing so such places are limited in world.
12. What do you understand by conversion of energy?
Ans-
It is a known fact that energy is neither be created nor be destroyed it can only be converted to one form to another. Because we can't create energy we have to convert energy available to us to the form that we need.

So the process of converting energy from one form to another form is called transformation of energy. In energy conversion 100% energy is not converted, some energy gets wasted in the process of conversion.
For exm.- 1) heat energy to electrical energy. (2)electrical energy to kinetic energy
In these cases -1 some heat gets wasted heating the machine and in case-2 also some electrical energy gets wasted into heating the machine.

Extra

Q-1) two uses of wind energy?

Ans-

1) the kinetic energy of wind to produce electrical energy by windmill.

2) kinetic energy of wind is used to produce motion in boats.

Q-2) what is solar cell panel, state its utility.

Ans-

Solar cell panels convert sunlight into electricity using photovoltaic cells. They provide renewable energy, reduce electricity bills, promote environmental sustainability, and support job creation. Their low maintenance costs and potential for energy independence make them a valuable energy source.

Q-3) explain bio gas plant with diagram.?

Ans-

- Feeding the Digester: Organic waste is mixed with water to create a slurry, which is introduced into the digester.
- Anaerobic Digestion: Inside the digester, anaerobic microorganisms break down the waste. The process happens in multiple stages: hydrolysis, acidogenesis, acetogenesis, and methanogenesis, which ultimately produce methane and carbon dioxide.
- Biogas Collection: Methane (CH_4) and carbon dioxide (CO_2) rise to the top of the digester, where they are captured as biogas.
- Utilization of Biogas: The biogas can be used as fuel for cooking, heating, or in gas engines to produce electricity.
- Discharge of Digestate: The nutrient-rich slurry that remains is removed from the digester and can be used as a bio fertilizer in agriculture.

END

www.ingramcontent.com/pod-product-compliance
Ingram Content Group UK Ltd.
Pitfield, Milton Keynes, MK11 3LW, UK
UKHW062008290726
14090UKWH00022B/1450

9 798896 104407